SOUL SOLITUDE

Taking Time for Our Souls to Catch Up

Rhoberta Shaler, PhD

G. Charles Andersen, MA

Humana Publishing

Rhoberta Shaler, PhD
G. Charles Andersen, MA
SOUL SOLITUDE: Taking Time for Our Souls to Catch Up
ISBN: 0-9711689-9-7

Cover design and book layout by somethingelse web+graphics,
www.time4somethingelse.com

First Edition: First printing, 2008
Printed in the United States of America

Published by Humana Publishing, San Diego, CA

For information, contact:

The Humana Center, Encinitas, CA
Website: www.HumanaCenter.com
Email: info@HumanaCenter.com

SOUL SOLITUDE

Taking Time for Our Souls to Catch Up

Dedicated to our families and loved ones who inspire and teach us, especially Brian and Luka.

Contents

When you recover or discover something
that nourishes your soul and brings joy,
care enough about yourself to make room for
it in your life.

- *Jean Shinoda Bolen*

INTRODUCTION

"FLAT-OUT IS NOT A RHYTHM!"

*Y*our mind may quickly agree with the truth of that statement. Yes, flat-out is not a rhythm. But, are you living flat-out anyway?

What we know and what we do are often not in accord. Where did we ever learn that if we ran as fast as we could, and then ran a little faster, somehow we might just catch up with being good enough? It could be that somewhere along the line, you, like many others, may have accepted these ideas:

- Running as fast as you can will make you a better person
- Keeping up the pace set by others is a requirement
- Losing yourself in a blur of activity equates to having a life
- Eating fast food is a wise nutritional program
- Comparing your life to others' is a reliable measure of success
- Strife and struggle are the price you pay for what you want

Do any one of those things give you a sense of control in your life? We strive and long for that, it seems. One thing is very clear: those things will not give us a sense of balance and stability. It may be time for a change in our thinking.

Running as fast and as long as we can is a sure-fire prescription for exhaustion on every level—physical, mental, emotional, spiritual. Some people have accepted this lifestyle to such a degree as to feel guilty when they *cannot* sustain the pace, when they really *should not* sustain the pace.

Our high-paced western culture sends us this message: we are simply not allowed to break down, to weaken, to succumb—even to bacteria or viruses, apparently. Years ago, there was a full-page color ad in a women's magazine that showed a mother with three kids. She was dressed in her business suit with briefcase in hand, marshalling her children into the mini-van to go to school. She looked cheerful and determined as she smiled for the camera. The ad said:

> *You don't need to slow down. Take [our medicine] and no one will even know you have a cold.*

What now? Is actually appearing to be less than perfect while juggling a life complete with kids, job, and dog something we should feel guilty about? That's the way it certainly seemed.

> *Don't let down the team. Don't even let them think for a moment that you are less than invincible. You must be Teflon Woman!*

That was years ago and the ad is long gone, however, the push, the drive and the pursuit has not been reduced. You know that's true by checking the late night ads for pharmaceuticals.

Our culture of go-go-go advocates denial. The advertising world makes billions selling campaigns for remedies, fixes and cover-ups to keep you in the game. We even borrow a war metaphor to compliment each other.

You're a real trooper!

We say that when someone hangs in, continues past the point of reason and in the face of daunting odds and questionable wisdom. What is that about?

It is no wonder that we have sleep disturbances, weight problems and a culture dependent on the pharmacy. Many people would rather take a pill than exercise or improve their diet. We like instant gratification . . . and results! And, we seldom allow ourselves to think about the quality of our lives in the moment. It's all future-paced.

One day I will . . .
Someday I'll have . . .
There will be time later for . . .
Not now . . .

What if this were the last day of your life? Your partner's life? Your child's life? Would you make the same choices you are making today?

WHY SOUL SOLITUDE?

It will give you a new view, a new attitude, a new approach, a new direction, a new start. Here you will find both the questions and answers your soul is waiting to hear. This book can change your life–and that of everyone you care about. It's in your hands now and that is a good start. Keep reading.

The Stumbling Block In The Stepping Stones

Are you tired of feeling pushed, pulled, harried and tense? It may have become the norm for you. Can you imagine it being different? Balanced? Clear? Focused? Relaxed? Successful on your own terms? It's possible.

One of the challenges that prevents folks, like you, from changing their lives from stressed to blessed is the transition period. It's like starting an exercise program. They don't want it to hurt, don't want to sweat, yet they want the results. It's not going to happen that way.

It's much easier, it seems, to have a reason why we cannot give up that "flat-out" lifestyle than it is to embrace an alternative one. That is, of course, until we come to the tipping point where we simply cannot run any more!

Would you rather wait for an illness, accident or breakdown than invite a breakthrough and embrace a better way to live?

Peace comes with a price: letting go of push, shove, hurry, must, should and ought to. It requires letting go of "keeping up with Jones'," "no pain, no gain," and, "give 'til it hurts." Are you ready and willing? You know that you are able. It's a choice. And, it's up to you.

You CAN make the transition from

> *I am running as fast as I can. Welcome to my world. Try to keep up, would ya?*

to

> *I am the author of my life and I live from my authentic self. I am creating my life, peacefully, with balance, harmony, mindfulness and joy.*

Why not construct your life rather than run after it?

The Predicaments

STOP!

- What would it take for you to choose to do that—
  to STOP?
- Would it be a big decision?
- Would you rather that your body makes the
  choice for you?
- Or, will you ignore it and have the regrets of not
  knowing where time went, or of someone's
  life passing you by?

**What Would It Take For You
To Take The Time For Your Soul
To Catch Up?**

Some experts—and popular magazines—suggest
slowing down. That could be useful. Many folks do
not listen very closely to that advice. But, is slowing
down enough? Will it eliminate the high cost of
running as fast as you can?

Here's a story that might help you understand that decision:

A police officer pulled over a red Porsche after it had run a stop sign.

"May I see your driver's license and registration, please?"

"What's the problem, officer?"

"Your just ran the stop sign back there at the last intersection."

"Oh, come on, pal. There wasn't a car within miles of me".

"Nevertheless sir, you are required to come to a complete stop, look both ways, and proceed with caution."

"You gotta be kidding me!"

"It's no joke, sir".

"Look, I slowed down almost to a complete stop, saw no one within twenty miles, and proceeded with caution."

"That's beside the point, sir. You are supposed to come to a complete stop, and you didn't. Now if I may see your license and . . . "

"You've got a lot of time on your hands, pal! What's the matter? All the doughnut shops closed?"

"Sir, I'll overlook that last comment. Let me see your license and registration immediately!"

"I will, if you can tell me the difference between slowing down, and coming to a complete stop."

The police officer had had enough.

"Sir, I can do better than that."

He opened the car door, dragged the obnoxious motorist out, and proceeded to methodically beat the roof of the car with his nightstick.

"Now sir, would you like me to slow down or come to a complete stop?"

(As found on www.PopuPlace.com, with thanks)

There is a big difference between slowing down and stopping! And, if you don't stop, nature may just shut you down and make you stop. Ready to choose?

HOW DID THIS RAT RACE BEGIN?

Tom Hodgkinson, author of *How to Be Idle,* says Americans can thank their cultural forebears, the Puritans, for instilling the idea that every single hour must be spent productively. For them, hard work was the route to salvation because it provided distraction from temptation. Heaven forbid, the mind and body could be still. Who knows what might creep in? Peace, contentment, a new idea, an insight? Wouldn't that be a waste!

Out with the absurdity of "idle hands are the devil's workshop" or any other lingering misconception that is creating a detour on your path to peace, creativity and understanding. Great relationships, worthwhile relationships, deep, supportive relationships require time and thought devoted to them. There is no way around that. It all begins with you. Start now to develop the supportive relationship you need to have with *yourself*.

Searching the internet for origins of the "rat race" terminology, a definition was offered of *competitive struggle to maintain one's position in life, especially at work*. Wow! Is that what all this is about? Are we really not even just rats in a maze in this metaphor, but rather, hamsters on a wheel struggling to survive in the game, and keep up?

The frenzied energy that the definition calls forth is very destructive and certainly anxiety-producing. Talk about being driven! How do you feel when you think that millions of people worldwide are in a competitive struggle to simply maintain their position in life? Picture a sea of hamsters on wheels. Where do you see yourself fitting in? Why?

And "keeping up" says nothing about another mighty stress, that of trying to "get ahead".

Are you becoming tempted to step off the wheel and assess your values and priorities? It seems to be a very wise decision. Of course, you could just keep running in step with your colleague or neighbor with a plan up your sleeve to bypass them in their sleep—and be willing to give up your sleep to accomplish it. If that sounds familiar, step off now before it's too late!

WAKE-UP CALL!

Behavior is simply you saying,

> *Look, world, this is who I am!*

There is no getting away from this fact no matter how many people will nod and say, "It's OK. I know. I know. There, there . . ."

Why do they give you all that wiggle room? So that you will do the same for them and neither of you will be called to attention or be required to look at behavior in need of a change. You are colluding to prevent change and positive growth: to stay the same with the same litany of "If onlys", "She done me wrongs" and "Ain't it awfuls." The drama continues.

Every word you utter and every action you undertake is a statement of your beliefs about:

- Yourself
- Others
- Your place in the world
- Your self-esteem
- Your confidence
- Your potential
- What you deserve
- How you deserve to be treated
- Your level of accountability
- Your degree of maturity
- Your values

Your behavior demonstrates your values every second, and shouts to the world "THIS IS WHO I AM!" There is no escaping that truth.

If you are reading this book, perhaps you already know you're ready for that wake-up call. Need another way to know for sure?

- You complain about the people you say you love
- You are very tired but you've had enough sleep

- You are fed up with making excuses to yourself and others
- You are tired of telling your story over and over
- You feel like an impostor
- You are exhausted on every level
- Your relationships are mediocre or unsatisfying
- You know there is much more to life and you're ready to find it

---

If any of these things are true for you, you are looking for Soul Solitude and the expression of your Authentic Self.
This book holds the keys for you to unlock that awareness in your life.

An American traveling in Africa hired a guide and a group of porters to lead him through the jungle to a remote village. Things went well on the first day. He was pleased with the progress.

In the mid-afternoon of the second day, the guide stopped and the porters set down their burdens and began to set up camp for the night. The American impatiently asked why they weren't taking advantage of the remaining daylight to make more progress towards their destination.

"We have traveled very fast and must allow time for our souls to catch up with our bodies," replied the guide.

PREDICAMENT ONE:
OUTSIDE EXPECTATIONS

So, we're rushing as fast as we can to a destination we think we want to reach using resources we may not have . . . and wondering why we feel pressured, disconnected and frazzled.

Who wants to think that our lives may be somewhat unexamined? We often get carried along by our families, our culture, the media, church, school and other sources of influence. When we were young, we accepted this as teaching, or at least, as what we needed to do to survive within those groups. Now, as adults, it is a worthwhile endeavor to examine our lives, motivations, contributions and drives once again.

There are two major predicaments to consider as we gently examine what is driving us in this life.

No matter where we come from or where we currently are, we have been introduced to the expectations of others . . . at a minimum. We may have been indoctrinated as well!

It is likely that we have done your best to meet those expectations in some relationships. More than that, we may have adapted, adopted or inherited the expectations of others for ourselves.

Whose Life Are You Living?

Napoleon Hill is said to have written these very insightful words:

> *I'm not who I think I am.*
> *I'm not who you think I am.*
> *I'm who I think you think I am.*

Another big question is: Who made you up? You could give some generally accepted answer like:

> *I am the product of all the people I have met and all the experiences I have had. Many people influenced my progress.*

And, you would be right if you could honestly say that you have been unconscious until this moment. No, not physically in a coma. We mean that you have been living your life on auto-pilot, retelling the stories that keep you stuck as the composite of your past. We know you might want to do a little special interest pleading right now on your own behalf. Sorry. It's time to take the leap to being a grown-up!

Follow Along . . .

As children we are shaped by the need for those giants in our life to like us well enough to keep us fed, watered and, hopefully, loved enough to survive. So, we listen, watch and take our cues from them.

Why giants? If you—a full-size adult—were a child right now, the adults would be seventeen and a half feet tall and eight hundred pounds. You'd be very likely to do whatever you needed to do to keep them on your side, right? That would be wise.

Now that you're an adult, though, have you re-thought your values, desires, preferences and choices so that they reflect your true nature? One thing is true: most people keep doing what they are doing and hoping for a different result. It has been suggested that this is the definition of insanity. The good news is that you can change at any time.

Whose Expectations Are You Fulfilling?

Are you living the life of your dreams . . . or someone else's dreams for you?

Is there a parent lurking in the back of your supposedly grown-up mind that you are still hoping to please by meeting their expectations?

We don't take this question lightly, nor are we suggesting that some parents don't have the best interests of their offspring at heart. Parents often can hold a vision for their child that the child cannot currently see and an identity that honors his or her best self. This is healthy as long as conversation is valued and individuality is honored.

Rhoberta had an experience that really opened her eyes to something that was holding her back. She has shared it in her keynotes and seminars and sees a majority of nodding heads. Perhaps it will have meaning for you. Here's the story in her words:

My mother had recently died and, as an only child, I fell heir to all her possessions. My father had died five years before.

Among those possessions were countless photographs. I decided to create photo albums for my three children going from the first days of my parents' albums through to the present moment. As I completed the task, with hundreds of photos arrayed on the floor, I remembered my mother's frequently-uttered words:

"It's a good thing you're smart, young lady, because you are too fat and ugly."

I know. It's unbelievable to me, even now, to think that she said that. So, I decided to look through those lifetimes of photos for evidence of "fat and ugly." Search as I might—and, of course, I could have a jaundiced eye—I could find nothing to support that as a fact. That was good.

Being a psychologist, I then became curious about why I went searching for the evidence. What came up might interest you.

There was still a part of me waiting for the approval of my mother. That in itself was of value, however, it got better.

My mom was a very uptight, rigid, judgmental and fearful woman who had, unfortunately, received many electroshock therapy treatments. She had strong opinions, a negative attitude, and racist views. None of which endeared her to me. The great gift that came as a result of this album-building experience was this:

> I was waiting for the approval of someone of
> whom I did not approve . . .
> and trying to live up to her expectations!"

This discovery would be heresy in some families perhaps, but for Rhoberta, making that connection was very freeing. Those Outside Expectations ended there. It was not necessary for Rhoberta to accept or attempt to meet her mother's expectations of the world, her family, her career, her church . . . or her daughter.

As healthy grown-ups, we are each free to choose to live from our unique Authentic Self rather than from any inherited script to meet the Expectations of Others.

In the seventies, there was a popular phrase:

If you love something, set it free;
If it comes back, it's yours.
If it does not, it never was.

Set yourself free of Outside Expectations. You have the opportunity of *a* lifetime and it is yours to choose how to invest. There is a big difference between spending a life and investing it!

Is there a possibility that you are waiting for the approval of someone of whom you do not approve? That can be a very draining use of energy, a low-level leak that can go unnoticed for a lifetime, leaving you debilitated and depleted.

When we are living from unexamined adopted, adapted, and inherited values, we are holding ourselves back from the life we were born to live.

That's why discovering your instinctual "hard-wiring" is greatly beneficial. It empowers you to live from your purpose alone.

One remarkable way to begin that process is to use a practical tool that helps you quickly learn and understand more about yourself. Taken online in only ten minutes, this tool gives you insights into your core nature, the contribution you intrinsically want to make and the strategies you naturally prefer to use. The insights extend to understanding your relationships, the people you live with and work with, and what you value most. It also offers valuable insights into your communication, fears, anxieties and conflict management approaches, which makes it an excellent tool for the workplace as well. With all those benefits, the Core Values Profile™¹ is just the right instrument to help you enlighten your journey of self-discovery.

WHY ARE CORE VALUES IMPORTANT TO CONSIDER AND UNDERSTAND?

That's easy. Core Values are the basis of your life: your beliefs, behaviors, thoughts, words and actions. Beyond the powerful information the Core Values Profile provides are the guiding principles you actively—or passively—choose to live by. Whether you consciously choose each one and are aware of your path, or, you drift through life unconsciously, you are broadcasting your core values to the world.

As a psychologist and motivational speaker, Rhoberta has seen many men and women who have not recently had a good look in the "360° Mirror of Life." They run on auto-pilot and away from self-reflection. These are the folks most likely to never let their souls catch up.

Here's an idea that is important to consider:

Your behavior IS your belief.

For some, that is a controversial statement. They want to argue with it vehemently.

No, I know better. I'm just lazy.

I am going along with the crowd. What harm is that?

If I can get away with it, it must be all right.

I would do things differently if only _____.

I never got the breaks in life that other people had, so . . .

If you had to walk in my shoes, you would understand.

So, what about the Outside Expectations in your life?

- Are they carefully examined?
- Are they old, worn or inherited?
- Are you ready to give up the outside expectations?
- Are you ready to create life from inside wisdom?

Is it possible you surround yourself with supposed friends who are actually operating from a hidden agenda—colluding with you to keep the misery going while experiencing misery loving company? Yes, it certainly is possible. And, like most folks, you have a range of reasons why it cannot be any different, usually beginning with how you will disappoint someone else.

- Who are you living for?
- Whose dreams are you living?
- Whose expectations are you fulfilling?

- Whose approval are you seeking?
- Whose needs are you meeting?

Big questions! AND, they NEED answers.

A man who trims himself to suit everybody
will soon whittle himself away.

- Charles Schwab

Of course, this applies to women, too.

IS IT BEGINNING TO ADD UP?

You construct your life. You decide what you value. You decide what you believe. You choose what you think, say and do.

If you are thinking that now is the time for you to claim your soul and live authentically . . .

YOU ARE READY TO TAKE TIME
FOR YOUR SOUL TO CATCH UP!

---

1. You can learn more about the Core Values Profile and experience the value for yourself at www.CoreValuesProfile.com

PREDICAMENT TWO:
ADDICTION TO DRAMA

*O*h, how we love our stories!

You likely have many stories in your repertoire: stories of joy, hardship, relationship, challenge, issues, ongoing struggle, breakdowns, and breakthroughs. For many, their stories become the fabric of life. They are simply stitched together and we think they are our identity.

No! Cobbling together a series of emotional vignettes is not a life story though many believe it is. It is a drama complete with characters, conflict, emotions, action, dialogue, often served up in theatrical style. It is designed to capture the audience and create a desired response—sympathy, empathy, upset, agreement or collusion. If we can engage someone in our story, in our drama, then, we have succeeded. After all, how could you expect a different result in life with that story? Poor me!

While the recitation of past drama goes on, there cannot be a focus on a new possibility. While we are recounting the difficulties, we cannot be creating new opportunities. While enmeshed in the past, we cannot be engaged in the present. It's that simple. Drama keeps us free of possibilities and opportunities.

We simply cannot be living in the past and also be in the present.

How "Addiction To Drama" Shows Up

- Do you have people in your life that like to create drama?
- Do they like to stir up energy and conflict, adding fuel to the fire and then dancing in it, relishing the flames licking at their feet?
- Do they retell the story for every willing listener?
- Do you know a man who is repeatedly late for work and known for extending coffee breaks into lunch hour but is surprised when he loses his job?
- Do you know a woman who thinks a man is giving her love taps when he hits her and she repeatedly offers excuses, forgiveness and another chance?
- Do you know people who just cannot stand life when it is peaceful and progressing easily?
- Do you know people who are happier when others are sad, hurt or depressed and really, really need them?

- Do you know someone addicted to "reality TV," who wants to keep you up-to-date on the gritty details?
- Do you know someone who always has a reason from the past for the failures, impossibilities or hopes for the present and future?
- Do you know someone who is always malcontented?

Whether we are engaged in it personally or vicariously, it's still drama. These folks are Addicted to Drama. They would likely protest that statement mightily. Evidence in reality, though, is different.

Families can be Addicted to Drama. No one would know what to do without it, much less know who they are. If yelling, anger, intimidation, put-downs, belittling, discounting or threats are the usual fare of family interaction, that's a family ready for prime-time television on the reality channel. And, then, think of the millions who would like to watch! All Addicted to Drama.

WHAT ABOUT YOU?

Who would you be without an "Ain't it awful?" or "He done me wrong" story to tell? Or, without the unhappy home and miserable childhood epic? Or, without the "You'll never guess what happened next?" intrigue. Is life an unending saga of victimhood and sabotage?

If you are thinking that we're talking about someone other than you, it may be true. Or, you may be experiencing a little denial or fear. What if that is you? What would that mean right now?

That might sound dire, however, it is worth considering. Because of a generalized Addiction to Drama in our culture, we may need to be focused in our consideration of our own lives. It seems so natural . . . because everyone is doing it.

JUST A WORD ABOUT DENIAL . . .

- We all experience wounding in life.
- We likely experience betrayal.
- We may be rejected.
- No one's life is continuously on the upward path.
- There are ups and downs, and hopefully, more ups.

Sometimes there is a dark night of the soul, a time of seemingly endless despair, hurt or confusion. Those times offer us two options, tearing us down and/or waking us up. It's all in the attitude, approach and understanding.

Denial is easily confused with positive thinking. The difference, however, is clear. Denial occurs when you refuse to see reality. Positive thinking is used when you can clearly see reality and choose to express your understanding of a better present and future. Pollyanna has nothing to do with it.

Denial is the refusal to acknowledge the existence or severity of unpleasant external realities or internal thoughts and feelings.

When they go unacknowledged, we are behaving from them subconsciously. Denial insures that we will not learn and grow, change and succeed. It keeps us stuck and we will argue vigorously for our limitations.

After all, fear arises when you have no identity without the drama.

Denial has a reasonable use. It can keep us from other kinds of misery. What if you had to acknowledge that your parents were dysfunctional and perhaps could not love you? That would take some time—and help—to work through. What if you were abused and finally began to understand that it was not your fault? Your life would change as your self-esteem returned and blossomed.

Do not let denial keep you from optimizing your potential and having the life you deserve. Look at the drama you've participated in because, even if you think it was *done to you*, you are continuing to participate every time you tell the story. Stop!

THE DRAMA CONTINUES . . .

Buying into drama, yours or another's, can happen so subtly, so naturally, that it goes unnoticed. The subconscious accepts the story and the habit is created. Until this moment, it might never have been uncovered or challenged, craftily masquerading as reality in your own mind.

The joy that comes from uncovering, discovering and discarding the drama is unparalleled. Once you are conscious that you have been unconscious, you may never be unconscious again. The blinders are off.

Family patterns have great emotional impact that is seldom seen for the disturbance it truly can be. The patterns are charged, highly volatile . . . and, they do not like to be touched! One of the "rules" of family drama is that it is to be unquestionably accepted by all concerned as truth, reality, the way things are. When you step aside, off that stage, and become an honest observer, only then can you see that the drama may well have been a horror story.

Of course, it would be wildly inaccurate to suggest that all families contain horror. Many are pleasant, nurturing places with happy memories. Many more are not. Yet, we know our roles and we slip into them easily, if not happily, when we are among our family. It is a story we know and a role with which we are familiar. But, are we addicted to the family drama? Would we be willing to step away from it to have a life in which the Authentic Self can flourish, prosper and fully optimize its potential?

Walking in Soul Solitude will help you decide. As you will discover as you read on, there is a much better path leading to a much more fulfilling, peaceful destination than the circular, adrenaline-rich and endlessly righteous Addiction to Drama.

AWAKENING TO THE DRAMA

Addiction to Drama is strong and compelling. So powerful that you can spend thousands of hours and dollars pursuing weekend seminars only to find yourself pulled right back into the drama you intuitively wanted to escape. Even the quest for transformation can become a drama.

Consider this scenario that we have heard so many times:

I was willing to do whatever I could to change my life, to be open to new ways. I took day, weekend, and week-long courses. I invested thousands of dollars. These things don't come cheap, you know.

Let me tell you what I have done . . . and you should do it, too. Have you tried . . . ?

It sounds benign. It can be perceived as a desire to help.

The real questions come:

- Have you taken the time to internalize the learning and improve your life?
- Are you happier, clearer, more peaceful and fulfilled consistently over time?
- Do you have a purposeful sense of who you are and what you are here to do?

These are not simple questions. If the answers are not affirmative, what was the point of spending the time and money participating in so many seminars? Many could transform their lives. But, do they? The change, motivation or insight lasts for a short while and they return to the familiar routines, behaviors and limitations. They regale their listeners with all that they have done as though the time and money spent were the reward, rather than significant life changes, improving their self-esteem, satisfaction and success. It makes great conversation and portrays an illusion of growth. That's not helpful, but the *Ego Self* is pleased.

There is no need to create drama in the quest for Dharma. Perpetuating drama by telling extensive stories about our quest for Dharma defeats the point. Focus on the questions above and move in the direction of a positive response.

Drama can be exhilarating and exciting when it is occasional, breaking up the seeming monotony of a peaceful existence. When it is basic to our way of being in the world, it leads to feelings of uncertainty, confusion and panic. It can also be frighteningly destructive, paralytic and absorbing. Who has time for their souls to catch up when they are consumed by what those Addicted to Drama see as immediate and imperative? Drama is a cruel master.

A Quick Test For Drama Addiction

- Do you happily repeat stories from your past that are filled with issues, challenging circumstances and allusions to being victimized?
- Have you struggled for years to get it all together and then keep it that way?
- Do you often feel that if you could just once get organized your life would change?
- Does life feel like a roller coaster ride over which you have no control?
- Do you seem to attract problems?
- Do you think others are causing those problems or your unhappiness?
- Do you often feel victimized and/or abused?
- Do you feel like you are a character in an assigned drama rather than the author of your life?

If you saw yourself in these questions, it is time to consider alternatives to the drama that fills your life.

As you understand and practice the thoughts of Soul Solitude, you can release the drama and realize the potential within you. You will free the energy that has been consumed by drama.

Imagine this scene:

> *A person gives you a $10 bill and asks you to hold onto it very tightly.*

> *To that same hand, the person then extends a $100 bill. You are unable to grasp the $100 bill because you are so tightly holding the lesser amount.*

That's the way it is with drama. If we are holding it tightly, then we are unable to turn our attention to other things. We cannot expand our awareness and consciousness into understanding who we really are and what our purpose, our dharma, is. We can only release ourselves to our potential when we are no longer bound by drama.

A WORD ABOUT FUN...

Spontaneity and play are the enemy of drama because there is no script for fun.

Think of the money, time and energy you have previously used to "plan to have fun." Perhaps it was in the form of an expensive vacation, a ski holiday, or the investment in a boat or summer cabin. Did planning to have fun work for you? So many people lament that the vacation did not live up to expectations or the cabin and boat became holes to pour money into- and no fun was had! It is frequently disappointing to plan to have fun. Fun just happens. It is a spontaneous occurrence, seldom pre-meditated.

And, so, it becomes drama. You return with stories of high expectations and less than acceptable results, with stories of who did what to whom and who is responsible for the trip being less than wonderful. And, then, you likely still have to pay for it!

That keeps us in the past once again. Have you ever had success in changing the past? Likely not, however, learning from it and moving forward has value. Any time spent in recrimination, regret and regurgitation is a waste. It is high drama.

DRAMA IN RELATIONSHIPS

For now, we can think about the anxiety and drama that relationship creates, particularly a romantic relationship. It is all about performance, and, therefore, there is little question why the divorce rate is unreasonable.

The drama of getting dressed up to go on a date, put our best foot forward and make a good impression can be heart-stopping. Couple that with our anxieties about what the other person may be thinking, feeling or noticing and the likelihood of a good outcome plummets. We are performing for each other. No one is being real, being his or her Authentic Self.

Slowly, the façade melts as it has to do. Keeping up the performance is too all-encompassing of time and energy. The real behaviors, thoughts, opinions and past surface. Many say that this can occur because we are now more comfortable with the new relationship.

What about being ourselves from moment one? Do we think we are not good enough in our usual state? What's going on here? Is it possible to dress like folks from Vogue and GQ while sitting in a five-star restaurant deftly managing five forks and knives and not slip into performance mode? If so, great.

If not, let's get real. It is just drama heightened to unreasonable levels.

Living in drama is often performance-based whether you are the performer, or you are judging the performance. And, you can certainly be addicted to either.

This subject of relationships is covered well in our onsite seminars where there is more time and individual direction. For information, visit www.HumanaCenter.com

THE PROBLEM

*W*hether we are Addicted to Drama or dancing to Others' Expectations, there is a fundamental problem that is common to both. In the Soul Solitude Workshops, we encounter considerable resistance to this point, until we unpack the situation a bit. Perhaps you also will resist the assertion that underlies the problem of Drama and Expectations. If you have been involved in either predicament, there is an inescapable conclusion that can be drawn:

YOU DON'T MATTER.

There is simply no nice or positive way to state this.

Often people object to this assertion and come back with some response that demonstrates they really do matter. Unfortunately, almost all the ways people demonstrate to themselves how much they matter involves some form of self-destructive behavior that underscores just how little they truly do matter to themselves. Whether it is indulging in a secret bowl of ice cream or drinking or smoking or other behavior they think demonstrates self-indulgence, such clandestine pleasures almost always involve a basic reinforcement of how little we matter to ourselves.

How can we matter if we are engaged in a headlong rush toward self-destruction?

WHY IS IT YOU DON'T MATTER?

Self-care is the most basic spiritual skill and is the basis of Soul Solitude. Because you do not really matter to yourself, you have resisted or sabotaged all attempts at personal change and transformation. This may be a shocking situation, but it is really important. Your ego will dispute this question and instantly respond:

What are you talking about? Of course, I matter!

All we can say is,

If you matter, why is your life so frantic, frenzied, frustrated, frazzled and/or frozen?

Soul Solitude is for people who matter to themselves. Our hope is that we can help you further develop this basic life skill.

First, we must cover some really important territory. There are three aspects to this:

1. Who am I?
2. I am not my circumstances
3. I am not who my script says I am.

WHO AM I?

*W*e have found that many people think a lot *about* themselves, but many of the same people, unfortunately, do not think much *of* themselves.

Large numbers identify themselves with a particular role or circumstance in which they find themselves, such as a profession or function—"lawyer" or "mother" etc. Later, we will sort out that situation, but for now, the question is about knowing ourselves without reference to some external aspect of life.

When we sit alone in the dark, we are neither role nor function, possessions nor circumstances. It is in that deep knowing without reference to activity or expression that we must struggle to center ourselves.

The model we are using for this journey suggests that the "I" involved is actually two different aspects of our being. The one aspect, which we will explore most, is what we call our "Authentic Self" or synonymously, our "Soul." This Authentic Self is the Soul that was brought into the world before we were conditioned or taught how to be. At this level, all are equal. No one is superior or inferior, but equal in all regards. Things like genetics and biology are merely circumstances that will influence our future as life unfolds. The Authentic Self resides almost exclusively in the deep sub-conscious, or our psyche.

On the other hand is the Ego Self which was not present at our birth, nor will it go on with us after we die. It is a temporal phenomenon, which influences how we are in the world.

The Ego Self is largely made up of projections and resides partially in our subconscious and partially in our everyday consciousness. Because of its orientation to the external world, the Ego Self is unable to look inward and therefore it concludes that it is the SELF and responds accordingly. The Ego Self is the part of us that we mostly identify with.

The Soul does not matter to the Ego Self which denies that it even exists. The Ego Self will resist all attempts at achieving Soul Solitude because, to the Ego, that is simply a waste of time (of which the Ego only has a limited supply.)

The Ego Self is necessary for being in the world. Some systems of belief treat the Ego as if it were the enemy. Our approach is simply that both the Ego and Authentic Self are necessary throughout life. Our Souls are present to learn and grow and the Ego is charged with providing the requisite experiences to achieve that goal. From the perspective of the Soul, experience is neither good nor bad, only necessary for learning and growth.

A model we have fun with is comparing the Ego and the Authentic Self to a monkey and a blind beggar, who travel together. The monkey dashes about trying to escape its tether to the blind beggar, and the beggar shuffles along, relying on his reluctant monkey guide and has no choice but to follow its lead. Ultimately, the best arrangement is when they travel hand in hand, walking with each other, supporting and sustaining each other with their particular gifts. That ultimately is the point of Soul Solitude.

So, in the still, sacred silence of Soul Solitude, the two aspects of ourselves encounter one another and possibly recognize and embrace each other in acceptance, gratitude, trust and surrender. The blind beggar holds and comforts the monkey, who finally achieves the comfort and recognition for which it has so vainly sought in the world of the external.

Who am I? Perhaps I am my Ego and Soul in conflict, or perhaps, I am my Ego and Soul in harmony.

Over-identification with the Soul can make us helpless in the world, which is ultimately unhelpful to the Soul, because it can only learn and grow by being fully engaged with the world, according to its capacity. Without a fully active and engaged monkey, the beggar just sits and withers.

Conversely, over identification with the Ego can lead to excess on many, many levels. The frenzy many people experience in their lives is a result of the tether being excessively long for the ultimate well being of the monkey. Too much dashing about, too many leaps and adventures without reference to the meaning and purpose of its existence can lead to self-destructive pursuits that neither satisfy nor fulfill.

When we address the question of "Who Am I?" we are looking into the deepest nature of ourselves. How we answer profoundly influences the question of whether or not we matter to ourselves.

If we are identifying with the Ego aspect, the Soul will not matter so there are simply no constraints imposed on the Ego. The Ego desires more. The Ego desires now. The Ego desires eternity. The Ego is God, at least to itself!

The Ego fears limits. The Ego fears death. The Ego fears the truth. The Ego fears consequences. The response of the Ego to fear is to run, fight or cower, or as we will discuss later, Shame, Blame, Judge and Justify. The Ego never considers context or consequences to its wants, needs or desires. The Ego is about doing, having, acquiring and keeping. The Ego loves drama—the more the better. Because the Ego requires limitless affirmation (and settles for so little), others can manipulate and control us with their faux appreciation. Because the Ego thinks so little of itself and has no context or appreciation of consequences, other peoples' expectations are somehow legitimized and blindly accepted.

We can begin to see how the essential nature of the question "Who Am I?" underscores the predicaments we get into regarding Drama and Expectations. We can further indulge the Ego by saying we are not going to allow others to control, manipulate or engage us in their drama. If we do not matter, such protestations are at best short-lived.

Even before we begin to legitimize our actions to
ourselves, we must deny the ego impulses that keep
us from silence and stillness. Only when we begin
to fully appreciate the dual nature of our being and
the dynamics at work in our life can we begin to
successfully operate from a position of self-caring.

We cannot begin to truly know who we are until we
engage in Soul Solitude, but engaging in Soul Solitude
will be challenging until we begin to know more fully
who we are. That is where a greater understanding of
the other two considerations that follow comes into
play.

I AM NOT MY CIRCUMSTANCES

*T*he pathway to Self-Care begins with the understanding that we are not our circumstances. Our life provides the context for our circumstances, not the other way around.

> *If only such and such a circumstance were different, then I could be happy or peaceful. But, with the rotten situation I find myself in, how could I ever be happy?*

As stated in the previous section, the nature of the Soul is to learn and grow from the various experiences it encounters as we engage in life. The Ego ranks experience as good or bad, wanted or unwanted. That is the nature of the Ego. The Soul just takes it all in and savors the experience. The Soul is indifferent to whether we are beautiful or rich or powerful. All conditions have things to teach the Soul. The Ego is in search of perfection and is continually frustrated.

Understanding the nature of "Who am I?" allows us to know that we are us in whatever circumstances we find ourselves.

If we do not derive happiness from our being, we will never know happiness from our circumstances.

Perhaps we might find fulfillment for a short time in changed circumstances, but such euphoria rarely lasts. Soon some glittering new circumstance shines before us and off we go to once again find fulfillment. Meanwhile, the Soul is fulfilled already, but we are so out of touch that we have no awareness or understanding of that. The monkey goes dashing off to find the treasure the Soul holds in abundance.

Often, when a person finds him or herself unemployed for any length of time, there is an alteration in their sense of well being. Fear and depression set in and they become locked in a self-referential cycle of shame and self-loathing that serves to increase the level of anxiety. The more anxious they become, the more ineffective in searching for a new job they become. While they are not their employment status, their lack of employment becomes the primary reality in which they exist. As the bills mount and the collection calls increase, the whole cycle becomes more intense.

From a spiritual perspective, there could be important insights learned from such an experience. Sometimes a breakthrough is preceded by a breakdown. Sometimes the monkey has to be wounded and return to the beggar. Perhaps an entirely new chapter of life could be unfolding, but the Ego shamefully and tenaciously clings to the past and limits the immense possibilities of life to just a few acceptable options. Perhaps a new job will emerge and the crisis resolves itself. However, there is a possibility that the Drama of unemployment may emerge again simply because there were lessons that went unheeded. In one sense, repetition of patterns can be seen as an invitation to learning.

Another area that affects many people is centered around their marital status. We will discuss relationships later in more detail, but the state of matrimony is not a "relationship", it is a circumstance based upon a relationship (or lack thereof). Chain marriages can reflect a pattern of unlearned lessons that indicate something new may be required. Inter-changeable partners are perhaps not the best teachers in such circumstances. Needing the circumstance of marriage is not the same as needing another person to the extent that anyone will probably fulfill the demands of the script. Meanwhile, the Soul craves contact with another Soul.

The Soul craves no circumstances. The Soul walks in abundance and fulfillment. The Soul seeks depth and intensity of contact with other Souls. The Soul needs no position of power or status—no recognition of accomplishment. The recognition the Soul requires is the deep knowing of "shared solitude" where trust is an unshakable bond, and light and peace flow in boundless measure. Any relationship that settles for less is probably a betrayal of the deepest part of our nature and is likely an "emotional trinket" of the Ego.

As we begin to know who we are, we begin to see how shallow the existence we have accepted for ourselves may be. We have tried to cram our Souls into what we call "Rice Paddy Circumstances," acres and acres of water but only a few inches deep. We settle for "Rice Paddy" relationships, jobs, and many other conditions. The monkey dashes about such rice paddies with reckless abandon, while the blind beggar sloshes through the muck and mire trying to find something solid to offer substance and support.

The message here is not to seek more substantial circumstances, nor is it to abandon any particular set of circumstances. The message is to not IDENTIFY with our circumstances. Because of the nature of things, those circumstances will change. We are called to be conscious of who we are regardless of the circumstances in which we find ourselves.

The implication for Soul Solitude is simply that we will not await some set of magic circumstances in order to attend to the business of Self-Care. We will begin now to matter to ourselves, and we begin by focusing on who we are, not where we are. From this spiritual perspective we are exactly where we are supposed to be, and all that we have experienced has been necessary to bring us to this "Golden Moment," this precious and irreplaceable NOW.

Hopefully you can begin to appreciate how necessary the awareness of "Who Am I?" is to the whole spiritual enterprise. As we more fully appreciate the gift and mystery of ourselves, we can begin the process of disentangling ourselves from the confusing morass of circumstantial misidentification. This process alone will help in diminishing drama and releasing us from the unrealistic expectations of others. We then turn to the complex problem of "I am not who my script says I am."

I AM NOT WHO MY SCRIPT SAYS I AM

With the advent of computers we have learned how useless hardware can be without the proper software to run it. The software contains a set of directions that determine how the computer will respond to any given set of circumstances. If the software encounters a set of circumstances for which it has no instructions, it either ceases to function or returns to some previous set of instructions that it could properly implement. Because of the nature of the Ego, it seems to function much like a computer.

We stated earlier that the Ego Self is largely a projection (inward and outward) of what its needs, wants and desires (expectations) are. In a sense, the Ego is a set of instructions for how to attain its expectations and how to respond if it does or does not encounter the desired outcomes. However, like all software, it will encounter unanticipated situations which require a novel response. Like a computer, sometimes the system is incapacitated and is paralyzed and unable to act. Sometimes it will fight and sometimes it will run. One of the things the Ego Self attempts is to never encounter novel situations.

In order to avoid the computer analogy, we use the language of "Scripts" to describe the algorithms or bits of wisdom that constitute our primary programming. Our scripts are not like Hollywood scripts that have been engineered to produce a finished product (film) but are conglomerations of bits and pieces of programming from many sources. We have scripts from our parents, our culture, our belief systems, teachers and many others who have influenced us, knowingly or unknowingly, over our lifetimes.

We express these various types of Scripts as:

- Those we have adopted
- Those we have adapted
- Those we have inherited

The most powerful of these are the ones we inherited, not only because they are the oldest but they are also the closest to us because we began picking them up even before we began speaking.

We learned how people and the world worked, or were supposed to work, by observing and interacting even before we fully acquired language. We adapted scripts from the people and situations we encountered as we grew up—sometimes from people we admired. In our teenage years, we adapted scripts from our friends and classmates, trying on behaviors and other expressions such as haircuts, clothing and music. As we became doctors, plumbers, fitness instructors, administrators, stockbrokers, firefighters and other "roles", we adopted the appropriate scripts for those roles. If we were drill sergeants, we adopted the persona of what the classic drill instructor was like. The same for teachers, nurses, and others. We adopted scripts for parents and spouses and then had to work out the differences between our script and our significant others'—if we could.

We will also refer to these scripts as our "active mythology"—which reflects the things we fear, desire and believe. Most people are unaware of just how powerfully these scripts and myths control our lives until a change in circumstances occur. The scripts persist long after reality has changed.

For instance, in the United States, the figure of the "Cowboy" is a persistent image that functions in a symbolic way for many people. Cowboys ceased to be an important function in our society well over a hundred years ago, but the cowboy mythology still dominates much of our psychic landscape as a culture. Shoot 'em up cowboy justice is still an operating part of the American Psyche, as demonstrated by events in our recent history.

Mythology persists, long after reality changes.

One of the things we mentioned above is that circumstances are subject to change. If circumstances change, but our scripts and myths remain, then we are subject to all kinds of things that, if they are examined, might seem rather incongruous.

For instance, there is the story of the woman who cut off two inches from each end of the Easter ham when putting it in the pan to bake. Her daughter inquired why she did that, and she replied that her mother had always done that, so she adopted that custom without knowing why. The woman inquired of her mother why she had always removed the two inches from each end of the ham, and the woman's mother laughed and replied that, at one time they lived in a house where the oven was too small to accommodate a full ham, so they had to remove two inches in order for it to fit into the oven.

This unexamined "custom" persisted from one house to another, from one generation to another.

It is the unexamined nature of the influential scripts of our lives that can be, perhaps, the most difficult to isolate and understand, particularly if there is an overriding pathology or dysfunction in our family of origin.

Children of alcoholics may be unaware at a conscious level, that their parent(s) drink in excess—so unaware that they may even defend their parent's drinking as reasonable behavior—because what is abnormal to others is perfectly reasonable and normal to them. Adults may often have trouble accepting the fact they were abused as children, mentally, emotionally or sexually.

Many of the scripts we have inherited, adapted or adopted have built in secrecy clauses—"don't tell or you'll regret it." Their power lies in the secrecy and isolation. Siblings dare not share, to insure that they not see the full extent of the control imposed upon them by decisions they never ratified or accepted.

Secrecy and silence insures that the script will continue. That is why effective counseling will often uncover toxic or dysfunctional scripts that interfere with the rational behavior of fully adult human beings. Those scripts will induce childish action in adults for no apparent reason.

One of the most common situations where this comes into play is when families gather. Suddenly adults will resort to patterns of behavior that were indicative of the way they interacted when they were children—without pause or consideration, the behavior just emerges. The existence and control of such scripts are frequently revealed at family holiday gatherings, such as Christmas and Thanksgiving. Many families experience dread or misgivings at holiday times because of the unpleasant occurrences that are blamed on the individuals involved and are rarely seen as effects of the toxic script that rules them all.

To understand that "We are not who our script says we are," is to take an immense step forward, because it breaks the cycle of shame and denial that protects it. When we can acknowledge the possibility that our decisions may be heavily influenced by programming of which we are unaware, we can begin the process of becoming fully conscious of whom we truly are. We may not consciously remember all the times we were called stupid, clumsy, fat, lazy or ugly, but those little snippets have been deeply imbedded within the programming of our lives.

In the mythic sense of "script busting", our approach is:

1. We need to know that we are living a myth.
2. We need to know the myth we are living.
3. We must actively choose the myth we want to live.
4. We must actively live the myth we choose.

This process however, takes root in the sacred, silent, seed-bed of Soul Solitude. It is in that place that we begin to clearly see the ubiquitous and corrosive nature of the scripts we have been living.

As we achieve consciousness of the affects that such programming has had on our lives, we can begin to free our Authentic Selves from the lies and poisons we have accepted for far too long. Drama is fed by our scripts, and the Expectations imposed on us are justified almost exclusively by unexamined scripts.

In preparing for Soul Solitude, we cannot examine all of the scripts that influence us. There are four we can look at:

- Shame
- Blame
- Judge
- Justify

The following are a few thoughts on these powerful, toxic scripts.

In the movie, *The Edge*, the primary character, portrayed by Anthony Hopkins, tells his fellow survivors of a plane crash that, in survival situations, the number one cause of death is SHAME. Those who find themselves in those circumstances cannot let go of all the "Shoulda, Woulda, Coulda's" of regret. The energy needed to deal with the demands of the here and now are diverted into a toxic mixture of shame and regret. They could have taken another flight, or wish they would have done something different, or should not have done such and such. Outside of survival situations, this problem may be even more common.

We all have regrets, but when those regrets become disproportionately powerful, we become filled with shame, which disempowers us to deal with the demands of the present. Shame can be paralyzing, and our culture is filled with it.

> Many people would rather find someone to blame for a problem than deal with the demands of actually fixing the problem.

"Who's to blame for this?" often seems to be a more compelling question than "How do we fix this?" Having someone to blame does nothing for anyone, but it does fulfill the requirements of a script. Hopefully, the person to blame is not us. If it is, hopefully we can find someone to shift the blame upon. If there is no one else to blame, then we must engage in damage control and spin. Accepting responsibility is not in the script.

Despite biblical injunctions against judging others, our culture delights in judgment. By making everything a competition, we actually justify our passing judgment upon others. There is no quicker way to feel self-righteous than to pass judgment on someone else and find them entirely lacking. Regardless of qualification, according to this script, anyone is entitled to pass judgment on another. Of course, it is a triple header if you can blame them, judge them and then justify your judgment about them—usually to their detriment.

From an Ego standpoint, everything we do, however cruel or unthinkable, is totally justified. Everything we do is perfectly reasonable—it is you who just cannot accept the reasonableness of my words or actions. Of course, if you make me angry, I am totally justified in speaking to or treating you in any way I feel is appropriate. Do not expect me to apologize, after all I am justified in my speech or behavior. The script demands that once you accept the reasonableness of my reaction, then I may or may not accept your apology. Whatever I say or do is justifiable, whatever you say or do is not.

The characterizations of these scripts may or may not sound familiar to you. We have found that they are very common among those people who have been caught up in Drama or Expectations. As we begin to hear these scripts operating in our lives, we can begin to examine and choose how we truly wish to be.

As we become fully conscious of the toxic and pernicious nature of these scripts, we can begin to free up energy that has been wasted maintaining such scripts long past their useful shelf life.

THE SHADOW PROBLEM

*O*ne of the brilliant insights of the Judeo-
Christian system, that became historically over-
theologized, was the understanding of human nature
reflected in the notion of Original Sin. Outside of the
story of the "Fall" was the underlying psychological
insight that there is something inherent in human
beings that creates an impulse to self-destruction.
Regardless of whether "eating the apple" was a good
idea or not, the story of Adam and Eve demonstrates a
truth that modern psychology has validated:

People do not always act in their own
best interest.

A major fallacy of the Age of Enlightenment was the
belief that human beings, if left to themselves, would
always act in their own best interest. Modern history
has given us many examples of just how wrong the

Enlightenment was. The newspaper is replete with stories of people not acting in their own best interests.

Carl Jung theorized that this impulse to self-destruction was a characteristic of what he called "The Shadow." Somewhere in the subconscious mind is something which compels us to sometimes act without regard to our long term best interest. Coupled with the problems of identifying with our circumstances or scripts, such an impulse can be very destructive to people, regardless of circumstances. People in high political office, such as former President Clinton, have been known to engage in activities which compromise the best interest of themselves and others. The Shadow respects no position of power, financial status, or claim to fame.

For instance, recently a prominent professional football player was convicted of gambling and dog fighting charges, seemingly ruining his career. Michael Vick had it all: professional stature, an enormous income, a promising future, commercial endorsements for years to come, and the respect of perhaps millions of fans; all the fruits of his years of conditioning and work. As is the nature of the "circumstantial", that all changed very dramatically. All that he had was not enough. For within him was the darkness of the Shadow. He lost it all, and may spend the rest of his life trying to recover what he lost.

To the Shadow, we do not matter. Michael Vick overly identified with his circumstances, thinking that somehow because of who he was and what he did, he was immune from the consequences of his actions. The Shadow blinds us to those things and compels us toward a cliff that few can avoid. Many may ask, "How could he let this happen? How could he be so stupid?"

From the perspective of Soul Solitude, the same type of thing could happen to any of us if we were in similar circumstances. That is the nature of things. Perhaps, while overcoming his indiscretions, Mr. Vick may have time for his soul to catch up. Others may not be so fortunate.

Eddie Griffin was a tremendously gifted athlete, who had great promise for an exciting career in the National Basketball Association. Things did not turn out so well for Eddie Griffin, who died in a fiery collision with a freight train—probably not accidentally. To his Shadow, Eddie Griffin meant nothing. All the promise, all the hype and all the expectations could not help him discover who he was. Drinking, drugs, fighting and indifference to the demands of his profession led to his demise, on an external level. The money, the notoriety and the other circumstances of his life could not help him find his way, and so he seemingly self-destructed—literally and figuratively.

The difficulty with the Eddie Griffin situation is knowing whether he over- or under-identified with his scripts and just what they might have been. Something eroded his path, and it crumbled beneath him. Whether it was his scripts or his shadow, he never had the time or opportunity to explore. The importance of taking time for one's soul to catch up cannot be overemphasized.

There seems to be an endless supply of drama mongers among the rich and famous. Because of their notoriety, their foibles are headlines for all to ponder and explore. They are parables for all of us, if we have the wisdom to consider their situations properly.

SUMMARY

Engaging in the central question of "Who Am I?"
we have encountered some powerful obstacles
to overcome in dealing with the predicaments of
Drama and Expectations. Hopefully we can accept
the notions that "I Am Not My Circumstances" and
"I Am Not Who My Script Says I Am." Accepting
these principles as valid ways of looking at ourselves,
perhaps we can begin to acknowledge that the
demands of Soul Solitude are important steps to giving
ourselves the Self-Care we need. While our scripts
will mitigate against such extravagant waste of time,
and the circumstances of our life will conspire to rob
us of the time and energy required for Self-Care,
Soul Solitude cannot offer compensation, but can
offer consolation for the sacrifices and compromises
required to allow our Souls to catch up.

Some of the things that Soul Solitude can do for us
are discussed in the next section. The Soul Solitude
Companion has helpful guidance for further exploring
ways we can help live a life of self-care.

THE PROMISE

*O*nce we become aware of how little we matter to ourselves and others, there is a very subtle shift that begins to occur in our minds and bodies. As we contemplate the reality that we are not our circumstances—nor are we who our scripts say we are—we will begin to experience a bit of upheaval. This is perfectly natural.

These powerful insights will disturb our equilibrium. We are all part of many systems; family systems, cultural systems, social systems, value systems and so forth. The nature of systems is that they tend toward equilibrium. When that equilibrium is disturbed, every system has mechanisms that will attempt to restore the system balance to what it was previously. We are no different.

Before going through all the possible turmoil that transformation entails, it might be helpful to have some awareness of what Soul Solitude promises, so we can consider whether the journey is worth the effort. In our experience, Soul Solitude offers four primary benefits:

FULLNESS

FREEDOM

CONSCIOUSNESS

JOY

FULLNESS & THE ARENAS OF LIFE

*A*s a result of our previous discussion, we know that we are neither our circumstances nor our inherited, adapted or adopted scripts. However, these things have been operating in our lives for a very long time and have forced us to live in a tiny fraction of who we truly are. Soul Solitude will help unfold the fullness we have been denying ourselves until now.

One of the most elusive questions that confront many people is:

What does it mean to be successful?

For some, success means lots of money. For others, success is a particular position or function or, maybe, a relationship. From the perspective of Soul Solitude, success is the full expression of who we are.

While "the full expression of who we are" may sound somewhat obvious, we have discovered that most people have no idea just how enormous their lives actually are. Because of our warped understanding of who we are, we have been content to live only a fraction of the full lives to which we were born. That is why we began with the question of "Who Am I?"

Soul Solitude is first, foremost and always about life. The soul is part of our lives and therefore is inseparable from any particular aspect. So, our journey to understand Soul Solitude is first about understanding the nature of the enormous lives we were born to live.

One of the models that we use to understand the nature and complexity of life is what we call the "Arenas of Life." This model consists of nine different arenas or aspects of what most humans can, or hopefully will, experience. These constitute a metaphor for the different aspects of a full life. The Arenas of Life are:

- Relationship
- Vocational
- Physical
- Creative
- Material
- Intellectual
- Circumstantial
- Recreational
- Personal

The various arenas work together in all aspects of what we do in our day-to-day activities. For the purpose of understanding, we make separations here. In reality those separations are not all that distinct in many of the things we do.

The Relationship Arena

This is the nature of person-to-person interactions.
What we like to call "soul-to-soul" relationship,
not "role-to-role" relationship. Within this model,
relationships have many levels of intimacy, honesty
and interaction. This arena is not about *roles* relating,
but *souls* relating.

The Vocational Arena

This is the arena of our professional life, the everyday
workaday world in which we engage our livelihood.
Many of us spend a lot of time focused on this arena.
Often, we try to cram many other aspects of our lives
into this arena, particularly relationships, creative life,
intellectual life and—because for many work is fun—
even our recreational life.

The Physical Arena

This is all about our bodies, including sexuality,
attractiveness, strength, health and all the other
physical aspects of being human. Often this area gets
neglected or minimized until our health diminishes
to the point that we can no longer ignore our bodies.
Conversely, many people obsess on their bodies to the
point they sacrifice fully living in all their arenas.

The Creative Arena

The Creative Arena is that aspect of life where we
explore that part of our nature that seeks expression
in the world. This takes the form of poetry, creative
writing, visual arts, inventing, gardening, acting or

any of a multitude of activities that we feel expresses, defines and identifies who we are. This arena can be somewhat intoxicating. History is full of examples of people who dwelt almost exclusively in this arena. This can also be an area of regret later in life, as we reflect on having left other arenas unexplored.

The Material Arena

The Material Arena involves the space and place we live in, the clothes we wear, our automobiles, as well as the way we keep up, improve and repair the various elements of our material life. Frequently, this arena demands considerable maintenance. This can be very problematic for a lot of folks because there are so many other things in life to do. For some, this becomes the basis upon which they judge themselves and others.

The Intellectual Arena

Reading books, doing crossword puzzles, playing chess or engaging in meaningful discussions are among activities which create new neural pathways in our brains. This is what the Intellectual Arena is all about. While many books are purchased, they are not always read. Courses begun may be abandoned. Learning a new language or other new skill can require a great deal of mental effort. For that reason, procrastination plagues this arena of many peoples lives.

The Circumstantial Arena

In terms of Soul Solitude, we give extensive consideration to the Circumstantial Arena. This arena is largely about the "structure" and "infrastructure" of our lives—the clubs we belong to, our families, our political affiliations, churches and all the other ways we express ourselves in the everyday world.

We can think of this as our "standing" in the community. Some aspects of the Circumstantial Arena include our wealth, our power, our fame and all the other attributes of status or structure we possess or that possess us.

The Recreational Arena

The Recreational Arena consists of those activities in which we actually re-create ourselves. Vacations, retreats and soulful activities are the primary substance of this arena. Unfortunately, many of us confuse entertainment with recreation and find that such activities become somewhat draining on our emotional lives. They can also become unhealthy preoccupations with energies and activities which are not in our best interests.

The Personal Arena

Finally, we consider the Personal Arena, which is the primary area of focus for Soul Solitude. This is the space in our lives where we get to be who we are and who we dream we are. This is an arena that contains secrets and hidden treasures which we hope to explore in Soul Solitude. While this is such an obvious and important area of our lives, it is surprising how little attention is actually paid to this arena.

The following diagram shows the relationships between the different arenas of our lives.

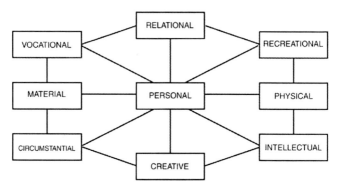

Fig. 1 - *The Arenas of Life*

As you can see, the Arenas of Life model offers a comprehensive picture of the enormity of even the most humble human life. The Ego Self has a difficult time dealing with such enormity. Part of the destructive self-indulgence in our rushing about is actually a purposeful neglect of many of these arenas.

We make ourselves so busy. We just do not have time to deal with those arenas. Week in and week out, year in and year out, they can lie neglected. That is, of course, until something breaks down and we are forced to bring balance back into our lives.

Soul Solitude promises to open up all the Arenas of Life and allow the Soul to walk in the vast landscapes of our being to which the Ego has denied us access. This is the fullness to which you are entitled, and to which Soul Solitude will give you the key.

Soul Solitude helps us to acknowledge the enormity of our lives, and to achieve rhythm, balance and synergy among all the Arenas of Life.

Because we simply cannot do everything at once, Soul Solitude introduces rhythm into our routines so we know that, in reasonably predictable ways, we are going to deal with the needs and issues of every arena in due course.

Balance (or more accurately "balancing") is what happens when the Ego Self tends to get over-involved in one or another of the arenas and neglect the rest. Proportional time and energy must be invested to bring about equilibrium when we spend disproportionate time in one arena or another.

Finally, synergy is about all the arenas functioning together, fully expressed. The temptation for the Ego is to frequently crowd several arenas into one in an effort to maximize time or energy. Unfortunately, this rarely works. To be open to the fullness of our lives, all arenas must exist fully expressed, all the time.

In terms of the demands of life, one of the phrases we are fond of using is:

Flat-out is not a rhythm.

There is no way that a person can go full-out consistently over a long period of time. The Arenas of Life model suggests that the only workable solution, which is what Soul Solitude is based upon, is Rhythm, Balance and Synergy.

FREEDOM

*O*nce we accept the notion that our lives are controlled by scripts, stories and myths, we can begin to free ourselves from those limitations that have been imposed on us. Since control is the very nature of our scripts, living a fully-expressed life is difficult for our scripts to control. They are evolutionarily developed to provide answers to all of the things we will encounter, in a limited sense. When we allow our Souls to go freely wandering about the various Arenas of Life, we are bound to experience things which go beyond the parameters of our scripts. Therefore, our scripts usually demand that we live a very limited life. In other words, "Do not live in your own Garden of Eden."

One of the truly important insights of Soul Solitude is that we cannot eliminate scripts from our lives. Scripts are inevitable.

Freedom is simply having a choice. We return again to the idea that, in the sense of Soul Solitude, freedom is in knowing these important principles:

- We accept are living a myth.
- We must know the myth we are living.
- We can choose a new myth.
- We can live the myth we choose.

Soul Solitude works by removing us from the rush-rush nature the Ego creates to shield us from knowing the scripts that control us. As long as we are scurrying about, there is no way we are going to be able to see how the scripts influence us so completely. Once we take the time to engage in Soul Solitude, the scripts begin to reveal themselves.

The Freedom that Soul Solitude offers is that of choice, not compulsion. Many people may think that not having to actively choose is a form of Freedom, and for them perhaps it is. We think that choice is preferable, but choosing requires that we be fully present to our choices. In other words, we become "mindful."

CONSCIOUSNESS

Within the context of Soul Solitude, Consciousness is the sense of being present to what we call the "Nearly Now." When we are present to our lives, without the rushing and tumult of day-to-day existence, there is a very different quality of life that emerges.

When we rapidly engage in the drama of past and future, there is an anxiety that sets in. When our scripts are listened to, they are filled with drama, dread of the future and regrets over the past. Being outside of the "Nearly Now," we encounter the scripts of Shame, Blame, Judge and Justify. Within the Consciousness of Soul Solitude, we experience no anxiety or fear, for in each Golden Moment is a power of peace and contentment that liberates us and allows us to be more effective.

The power of being fully present to our own lives is an untapped resource until we engage is Soul Solitude.

Incredibly, as we walk hand-in-hand with our two natures, we see clearly how to be more fully engaged in important matters and how to disentangle ourselves from the Drama and Expectations that others may try to impose upon us. This leads to an sublime sense of peace and joy.

JOY

*O*ur soul is an expression of divine joy. Our very being proclaims the wonder and mystery of creation. What makes us so special that the Universe needed to express or create us? Such expression has been anticipated since the dawn of creation itself. We walk in mystery and dance in wonder. Within the context of Soul Solitude, we get to experience and express that profound sense of wonder and joy. If that were not enough, as we become ever more fully an expression of joy, our transformation changes the people and situations around us.

Soul Solitude cannot promise happiness, immunity or escape from the difficulties and challenges that will face us. Soul Solitude will help us consider the landscape of our journey; the landscape through which our soul encounters the experiences needed for growth. That landscape is neither romantic nor sentimental, and we call it the *Dharmic Themescape*. The

Themescape suggests strongly that the nature of our journey is essentially:

PAINFUL

DIFFICULT

COMPLICATED

Soul Solitude cannot change the landscape of life. What Soul Solitude can do is help us cope with the fundamental nature of things as they are. Some people dispute our analysis about the "nature of things," because it contradicts much of the marketing language of the "self-help" world. Positive thinking advocates and others will tell you that, if you think negative thoughts, that is what you will receive. The misunderstanding is simply that the Themescape is neither positive or negative and is not subject to our mental energy. Like the desert, it exists on its own terms. Our suggestion is simply that it is better to accept the landscape as it is and not try to change it. Save the energy for the journey. Dealing with the landscape is far more effective than attempting to change it. There is joy, not necessarily happiness, in that landscape.

The following diagram is a graphic representation of the Themescape. For a fuller discussion, see Appendix Two.

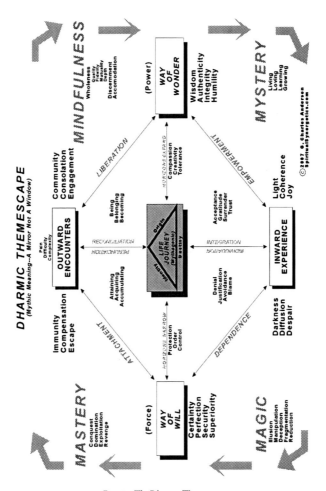

Fig. 2 - *The Dharmic Themescape*

We use this Themescape in virtually all of our work. It allows us to frame the discussion of Soul Solitude in reasonably coherent ways. We think that as you enter into Soul Solitude, this model will help achieve a level of consciousness that many people do not have. More will be written about that later.

So, the promise of Soul Solitude is that things will change. Life will be different because you will have a new consciousness of being in the world. The speed and degree of change, however, is not determined by our Ego. Part of the journey is to know that we are right where we need to be at each step of the journey.

As you undertake familiarizing yourself with the process of Soul Solitude, we are confident that you will begin to notice that the world has changed significantly. Others will notice. Be not dismayed when people and situations emerge that will try to tempt you back to a former way of being. From this point forward, things will be different.

THE PROCESS

$\int$o, here we are at the crux of the matter:

- What is Soul Solitude?
- Where is it found?
- What is the path from where you are to it?
- How will you know when you've found it?

We have written extensively around the topic of Soul Solitude to prepare for this understanding. You'll remember from earlier in the book the story about the policeman and the Porsche driver who was bewildered by the need to come to a full stop. As a demonstration of that difference, the policeman pounded on the Porsche with his nightstick and asked:

Now sir, would you like me to slow down or come to a complete stop?

Soul Solitude asks you to come to a complete stop. For many, the mind balks at that suggestion. When we are running, rushing, hoping to catch up, it seems almost counter-intuitive to stop. That is what is most needed.

Stop—Sit—Still—Silent Sacred Space

WHAT ARE YOU BUSY ABOUT?

We are busy. The world is busy. This is not new to the twenty-first century. It was no different, apparently, in Wordsworth's time when he wrote:

The world is too much with us; late and soon, getting and spending, we lay waste our powers: Little we see in Nature that is ours.

Or, more recently, an anonymous writer contributed:

Most people are so busy knocking themselves out trying to do everything they think they should do, they never get around to what they want to do.

We can be very busy and accomplish little. You can also be very focused and accomplish much. It is the quality of the time spent that produces the results. That is why it is imperative to focus on what we are truly busy about.

This is not about time management and yet it is all about time stewardship. Paradoxically, you will discover that choosing to sit in the Silent Sacred Space opens up time, clarifies priorities, harvests thoughts, changes direction and calms the body. Those things alone are worth the engagement . . . and, yet, there is more!

GATHERING THE THOUGHTS . . .

Throughout this book, we have strewn ideas that move towards Soul Solitude.

Understanding your "instinctual software"—the contribution you bring to the world and the strategies you prefer to use—through the Core Values Profile™ is a concrete, practical beginning. For more on the Core Values Profile, see Appendix One.

MINDFULNESS

*M*indfulness is a basic practice brought to attention by many traditions, most noticeably Buddhist. This is a moment-to-moment focus, consciously bringing the stillness of meditation into the thought or task at hand. Staying awake, aware and alert to the fullness of the "Nearly Now" changes the quality and texture of your day.

Patience is required for mindfulness to be present. Not only the commonly understood concept of patience but further understanding that, in the patience, there is a lack of judgment. For example, people learning to meditate become impatient with themselves. They feel sleepy. They lose focus. They peek at their watches. As they do these things, they have judgments about themselves, about the process and, even, about the teachers. There is no patience and much judgment. In Soul Solitude, this is released.

There is an internal stillness that accompanies Mindfulness; it is as though time stills with focus. There is only the moment. There is only that person, that ladybug, that sunset, that idea.

The most precious gift we can offer others is our presence. When mindfulness embraces those we love, they will bloom like flowers.

-Thich Nhat Hanh

And, so will we bloom. Mindfulness is an interactive gift, benefiting all.

SOUL

M uch has been written about the Soul, such a vast concept. It is wise to remember the story of the five blind men who encountered a single object all approaching it from different angles. Each described what they felt and each description was completely different. Each had found a different part of the same elephant. So it is with describing the Soul.

Another understanding of the concept of Soul may help to unlock the purpose and focus of Soul Solitude.

- What is it that we are truly connected to?
- Where is the Soul?
- What is the Soul?
- Where is our grounding?
- What is our source?
- What are our resources?

There are many deep definitions of soul, with a wide variety of opinions, from an equally wide variety of religious, spiritual and philosophical stances. Explore them if you are ready for more depth. For now, let's take two simple, more traditional ideas as a point of departure for our understanding of soul.

Webster's Dictionary:

> *soul - the immaterial essence, animating principle, or actuating cause of an individual life; the spiritual principle embodied in human beings, all rational and spiritual beings of the universe; an actual or essential part; a moving spirit; man's moral or ethical nature; that quality that arouses emotion and sentiment*

Your animating principle, that which is the deepest nature of you, your spirit, is called soul. To expand that definition, read what Dr. Dennis Merritt Jones[1] says:

> *The truth is there is only one Soul and it is the Soul of the Universe. Individual man's soul is simply that point within him where the Universe (or God) personalizes Itself.*
>
> *We believe that the soul is man's creative medium and is therefore subjective (or subject) to his conscious thought. The soul is that perfect part of our being which accepts us and our actions, never judging us as right or wrong, always ready to "assist" us in achieving whatever we choose to do when we believe we can do it.*
>
> *The soul has been referred to as the "mirror of mind" because it reflects the forms of thought which are given it. We choose the thoughts it reflects or, in other words, brings into experience.*

Thinking further about the soul as being perfect and part of each person's nature is a great beginning—no room for poor self-esteem as it is **clearly** just a thought that can be changed to create a **new experience.** Isn't that a relief?

You may have thought that your **poorer** thoughts about yourself—the ones you may **keep** hidden, the ones that you fear may escape or escalate when you actually sit down in silence without the television, book or person—were who you really are. No!! You accepted someone else's opinions and adopted them for your own. Thinking of yourself in a brand new, positive, uplifting and empowering way begins with your next thought. Choose it well!

In light of the two definitions of soul above, the questions become:

- Are you taking time for that perfect, creative part of yourself to choose the thoughts you wish to bring into experience?
- Are you taking time to determine who you really are and express yourself fully?

Or, are you so busy *doing* that you take no time for *being?*

We are called human beings, not human doings.

There is no time like the present to become present and invite your soul to catch up!

---

[1] Dennis Merritt Jones, R.SC.D. How to Speak Religious Science, DeVorss & Co., Marina del Rey, CA. 1999.

THE CIRCUMSTANTIAL

You are not your circumstances.
Your life is not your circumstances.

This distinction alone regarding the Circumstantial
can make an amazing difference in your life when you
fully accept it and live knowing it to be true.

As we indicated in an earlier chapter, much of our
busyness is the result of that misperception. As
you step into Soul Solitude, you can let go of these
childish things as there is no more need to confuse the
two.

REMEMBER THE PREDICAMENTS

Awareness of the roles played in our lives by Outside
Expectations and Addiction to Drama allows us to

---

reflect on the underlying principles and premises of our life and consider changes. For whom are we engaging in this life?

We spoke of the stewardship of time earlier. Each person has the opportunity of a lifetime that is segmented into one hundred and sixty-eight hours each week. We alone are the executive decision-makers regarding the investment of those hours. It is mindless to simply "spend" time. It is wise to invest it. This distinction allows us to consider the alignment between our values and our daily lives. If it is not there, the investment is minimal and the value we place on our lives is marginal. Our lives are about expressing our Authentic Selves and this cannot be done without full attention.

In all our work, we align ourselves with the sentiment Shakespeare expressed when he wrote:

> *This above all: to thine own self be true.*

We are unique expressions of the Divine. In order to live fully—optimizing possibilities and opening to opportunities—we believe that Soul Solitude is the bedrock, the foundation upon which we build. As the Bible says in Mark 8:36:

> *For what shall it profit a man, if he shall gain the whole world, and lose his own soul?*

We want the connection to self and God, that "Soul Connection" that it is found in Soul Solitude.

HOW DO I FIND SOUL SOLITUDE?

*A*s we were preparing this book, a facetious interview took place. One of us took the part of an Oprah-level host, the other of the guest and interviewee.

Host: *What is the first step in finding Soul Solitude?*

Guest: *Sit.*

Host: *Sit and do what?*

Guest: *Sit.*

Host: *That's it? Sit.*

Guest: *Yes, simply sit. Give yourself permission to simply sit.*
(Noticeable discomfort on the part of the host)

Host: *So, is there beginning sitting, intermediate sitting and advanced sitting.*

Guest: *No, simply sitting . . . and relaxing.*

Host: *How can I relax when I'm so uncomfortable with nothing to do?*

Guest: *Why are you so uncomfortable with nothing to do? Why are you so uncomfortable with simply sitting and being?*

Host: *It seems so unproductive. I could be using that time to accomplish something, strike something off my "to do" list.*

Guest: *Investing time to "be" is unproductive, then? "Doing" is what counts?*

Host: *Well, why am I simply sitting there?*

Guest: *To allow the mind and body to relax, to have no agenda, no plan, no particular focus beyond being.*

Host: *Well, how do I sit there? Do I sit in a certain way? Do I do something with the feet or hands or eyes?*

Guest: *You simply sit comfortably. You notice what thoughts spring up in your mind and observe them without judgment.*

Host: *That's difficult. All kinds of things might show up.*

Guest: *That's the point. To observe them without judgment and with interest, asking only the question, "For what might this be good?"*

Host: *(Intrigued) So, there is no technique, no pretzel-izing, no gazing, no mantra, no candle. You simply sit and entertain your thoughts with a positive interest.*

Guest: *That's it! Simply sit.*

Just like that host, we look for the ways to complicate the matter, to discover how we can fail. You may have experienced training in many forms of meditation, yoga, prayer, mind treatment and affirmation, as we have. Many people suggest there is a right way. Once we become concerned about doing it the right way, we are not focused on the practice. We're concerned with doing it right. The mind can only hold one thought at a time. It is a binary machine. Therefore, while concerned about doing it right, you cannot find Soul Solitude.

There is NO drama in Soul Solitude.
You cannot fail. There is no technique.

BEYOND SIMPLY SITTING . . .

*I*t might be that thoughts enter your mind from what we like to call the Voice of Inspiration. It's like:

Psssst! Have you thought about this?

No judgment. Entertain the thought. Ask only:

For what might this be good?[2]

In turning to this question and away from judgment, we open ourselves to new thoughts, new insights and new ways of being. There is no right answer once again. There is no script. There is no failure. Only interest, curiosity and expanded awareness.

In order to capture thoughts, ideas, insights and inspirations, we may find it useful to keep an open journal ready to record them. We may further wish to keep in mind "For what might this be good?" This way, we can consider them further while not interrupting the flow of thoughts while sitting.

There is no amount to write or a need to write, it is an option only. If something comes to us and we want to capture it accurately, we can. The mind is quite habitual and it may have a frequently-operating program that wants to edit, monitor or censor our thoughts.

That's the voice that pops up with:

Don't be ridiculous. That could never happen.

That's stupid. What are you thinking?

By capturing our thoughts in a few words or a diagram, we can focus on the possibility while reminding ourselves that each thought has a purpose and is worthy of our attention. While doing this writing, our focus is on the capturing, not on the constricting, limiting, habitual voice that wants to dismiss the idea.

If we are more visually-oriented than auditory, we may not "hear" the Voice of Inspiration, but rather be inspired by images. Again, there is no right or wrong way to simply sit.

If we find ourselves moving as we sit, that, too, is fine. Many people process information kinesthetically and need the movement. Remember, there is no wrong way to simply sit.

Trust yourself in the present moment. Trust yourself. Be open to the inspiration for yourself. There might be a tendency to go off to run the idea by friends. Resist this urge. This is for you. Entertain it well as possibility. Explore what is there for you.

When we share ideas with friends, let us offer a caution: choose friends who are open, like-minded, willing to explore and unlimited. When we have an expansive thought and we share it with friends living in judgment, habit and justify—or worse, living in shame, blame, judge and justify—they are very likely to give us all the reasons why we should not engage with it.

Too frequently, we share our ideas *while holding a secret agenda hoping to have them dismissed!* Be mindful of this. You are the author of your life. Friends can be wonderfully supportive, amazingly stultifying, or wildly competitive. Your thoughts are gems. Treat them as such.

WHAT THEN?

> Simply sit.
> Listen.
> Repeat frequently.

Simply sitting in silence is new for many people. Silence is such an alien concept. Radios blare. Bass speakers pound. People interrupt. Children have requirements. Choose a time when silence is most likely. You can have quiet instrumental background music if that helps without distracting. That is why we have worked with talented musicians to create the Soul Solitude CDs to offer inspiring, gentle, wordless music as a backdrop to your thoughts.

What am I listening for?

Nothing apocalyptic, really. Just listen. Listening is an activity in itself. You are not thinking of other things, making conversation in your head. You're not planning or dwelling on the past, present or future. You are simply being . . . and being open.

There are no Six Steps
to Soul Solitude Success!

Disappointed? There is no way to fail and no way to make yourself wrong. This might be a first for some people!

Simply stop, sit in the silence, relax and listen.

For how long?

Rhoberta was recounting a case study of an executive coaching client:

> *"You want me to just sit there???"*
>
> *"Yes, just stop, sit, relax and listen."*
>
> *"You simply do not understand how busy I am, how many things I have to do, how many people I am responsible for!"*
>
> *"Yes, I do. That is a distraction to sitting. Simply sit."*
>
> *(Big sigh!) "For how long?"*
>
> *"Begin with fifteen minutes?"*
>
> *"Are you out of your mind? I could be doing something."*
>
> *"That is the point. For those fifteen minutes, you are giving up doing and simply being."*
>
> *There was a silence.*
>
> *"That is simply scary. What if I cannot do that for fifteen minutes?"*

*"Begin with five. My experience is that, as you do this
simple practice, you will look forward to this gift you give
yourself and you will naturally want to sit longer."*

And that is just what happened. That executive is
functioning at much higher levels while experiencing
more honest happiness than ever before. Certainly,
it took practice and willingness. The rewards were
surprising—to him.

We get some very interesting perceptions about this
kind of activity. We believe there are noteworthy
differences, which we discuss in our seminars,
between Soul Solitude and meditation . If you have
studied meditation, you know that there are many
forms—each slightly different with different rules or
suggestions. Different people find value in different
approaches. One difference between meditation and
Soul Solitude, then, is the lack of technique, method,
accoutrement or requirement.

We suggest that you do not get caught up with the
time or technique involved.

You are a human being, not a human doing.
Simply be . . . and sit.

---

[2] This question was first introduced to us by a wise man in Calgary,
Alberta, Canada by the name of Maynard Dalderis. It has become a
primary focus on the path to Soul Solitude.

BYPASSING THE EGO SELF

*W*hen we give ourselves permission to sit for
ten minutes in silence, listening to nothing
but what's within us, we can bypass the Ego Self. No
longer will that chatter be about "I":

- I could be doing something different.
- I don't know what to do.
- I could be getting something done.
- I think this is ridiculous.
- I wonder how I look doing this.

The mind is still. The body is relaxed. There is
nothing else to do. Nowhere else to go. No one to
see, hear or find. There is nothing to master—no
technique, no method, no formula, no agenda. This is
our time.

WHAT IF I FALL ASLEEP?

That's possible. There is a good first and obvious
insight there: either you need more sleep or you are

avoiding self-reflection. Answer those questions and move on.

If we fall asleep, we will eventually have enough sleep. Then, we will sit silently and be . . . awake.

If we are avoiding self-reflection and are fearful of what we will find when we are so uniquely alone in this sitting, we need to explore this insight. The Companion that accompanies this book is an invaluable, practical resource to assist us in understanding ourselves more in this regard.

If we have been running as fast as we can to that elusive destination the world labels "SUCCESS", we may well need to take better care of ourselves. If we're running that fast, we may be concerned about what happens when we stop. That is the first step in entertaining a healthier lifestyle. We will be fine . . . and, so will the rest of the world.

If we think we are indispensable, we can simply put a finger in a glass of water. Remove it. And, observe the hole that is left behind!

Clearly, the world will not stop turning if we take time to sit and find Soul Solitude. It also will remain rotating on its axis if we make catching up on our sleep a priority—unthinkable though it seems!

One of the greatest causes of illness in North America is reported to be lack of sleep. Folks are running too fast, worrying too much and imagining the worst. STOP! Begin by catching up on your sleep. If you will not do that, with a litany of reasons why it is impossible, then know that taking the time to simply sit, relax and listen will have great benefits for you. You can train yourself to stay awake by becoming interested in your thoughts, insights and intuition. That curiosity will hold your attention and keep you awake.

And health on every level? What a great reason to take time for your soul to catch up!

SOUL SOLITUDE IS NOT A "SHOULD"

Soul Solitude is not a "should", not an outside imposed regulation that makes you a good person. It is simply a choice we make. We arrive at a decision to matter enough and realize that there are steps we can take to be healthy—physically, mentally, emotionally and spiritually. We engage in Soul Solitude because "we matter to ourselves." We might say to ourselves:

I matter therefore I . . .

You do matter, so therefore, put in place things that you know would make your life richer. Those may be better sleeping, eating or exercising, and/or, simply sitting in the sacred silence each day. Demonstrate to yourself that you do indeed matter.

SOUL SOLITUDE IS DIFFERENT

Soul Solitude offers a paradigm shift that is not about our usual adopted, adapted or inherited scripts. It is not about self-help prescriptions. People who engage in Soul Solitude want to be fully functioning, healthy grown-ups in a world that fails to encourage that.

When people insist on their Addictions to Drama and People Pleasing behaviors to create a lifestyle, it is not possible to become a grown-up.

- Grown-ups know there is no one to blame.
- Grown-ups have given up shaming, blaming, judging and justifying.
- Grown-ups take full responsibility for their lives— their thoughts, words and actions AND the consequences.
- Grown-ups know they create their lives and are the only decision-makers about their lives.

> **When we decide that Soul Solitude is an important component of our lives, that we deserve the sense of connectedness, peace and wonder that we find there, we will make taking time for our souls to catch up a priority.**

This is not a "how-to" book as much as it is an invitation to "want-to." It is a description, not a prescription. This is a description of the value, insights and impact you will experience when you allow yourself to simply sit.

> **Soul Solitude is a drama-free description, not a drama-filled prescription.**

If you happen to be wondering if you can bring yourself to the quiet of Soul Solitude, we invite you to view the movie, K-PAX. Folks with OCD (Obsessive-Compulsive Disorder) simply do not sit still waiting for something to happen. They respond to most stimuli in the environment and move much of the time.

Kevin Spacey's character encourages focus in a fellow who is an extreme obsessive-compulsive. He tells him that something amazing is going to happen when he sees the return of the first bluebird. No one expects to see a bluebird . . . and they expect the OCD person to watch for it even less.

Because of the encouragement Kevin's character gave him, the sense of expectation and wonder, the fellow did sit for hours and days watching for the bluebird. And, it arrived to the amazement of all concerned. However, the most amazing thing was not the arrival of the bird, but the stillness of the watcher—who transformed his illness simply by sitting.

It is similar with Soul Solitude. You sit. You relax. You listen. You pay attention. And, the bluebird appears! Perhaps not the first day or the second, but then, there it is—beautiful, inspiring, surprising, unbidden and appreciated, and all from your willingness to simply sit.

THE DOMINANT PARADIGM

We've mentioned that we are often living scripts created by Outside Expectations. We not only have Expectations but we also have Competition and Desperation. What a trio!

When we are talking about taking time for our souls to catch up, we must examine our scripts to find out

where the competition and desperation are welling up
from. It seems they come from the Big Three:

> Run as fast as you can.
> Have as much as you can.
> Do as much as you can.

Who wrote those rules? The better question is:
why are they operant in our lives? Let's not look for
someone to blame, just look for a straightforward way
to decide if they are right for us.

Not only do those rules "rule", there is a final step
in the process: follow the Big Three and "they"
will decide if you are good enough. It is as though
we believe there is some kind of universal clique
determining whether or not we're good enough. Good
enough for what?

As the bumper sticker says, "Subvert the Dominant
Paradigm." To do that, we have to make changes. Not
everyone in our lives will applaud those changes, so
be prepared. You will lose the approval of many who
are ruled by the Big Three. You may lose a few toxic
people who are dependent upon your desire to please
them. You will be happier, freer, more joyful. What's
your choice?

AND, AFTER SITTING, WHAT?

*T*here are four Soul-Centering Principles™ to keep in your consciousness on a moment-to-moment basis in order to sustain Soul Solitude. When you have accepted them as the focus for your purpose, your Dharma, you will be free. They are simple to remember, not always easy to sustain.

SOUL-CENTERING PRINCIPLES™

ACCEPTANCE

GRATITUDE

TRUST

SURRENDER

ACCEPTANCE

*I*n the context of Soul Solitude, Acceptance will be used in two distinct but related ways. They are circumstantial and spiritual. Both are essential to full and vital living.

CIRCUMSTANTIAL ACCEPTANCE

Circumstantial Acceptance allows us to free up energy that gets diverted when we engage in denial. In this sense, Acceptance allows us to effectively respond to what is actually happening around us. A few things are important to understand about Circumstantial Acceptance:

- We are not talking about tolerance of injustice or abuse.
- We are not talking about indifference to the world around us.
- We are not talking about acceptance of the status quo.

- We are talking about acceptance of the nature of
  things:
  > Pain
  > Difficulty
  > Complexity
- We are talking about acceptance of the fact that
  people can be:
  > Cruel
  > Unjust
  > Capable of doing horrible things
- We are talking about acceptance that this really is
  happening to me NOW:
  > Being told we have cancer or other life-
  > threatening illnesses or situations
  > Being told of the death of a loved one
  > Seeing the World Trade Center burning

Circumstantial Acceptance is seeing through the fog of denial and inaction, allowing us to think through the situation and working through an effective response to any particular set of circumstances. Sometimes there may be no effective response possible. For many trapped in the burning World Trade Center that may have been the case. Millions watched in horror and disbelief as person after person leapt to their deaths, exercising what little control they had in at least choosing their manner of dying.

Sometimes life confronts us with unimaginably awful situations and unthinkable choices. That is the nature of things, whether we like it or not. We can accept this, or become paralyzed when the unthinkable happens. If things can be changed, we will need all of our mental, physical and emotional energy to deal with effecting those changes. If not, we will need our wits about us to deal with just being present to the final beats of our heart.

SPIRITUAL ACCEPTANCE

Circumstantial Acceptance is a powerful tool for dealing with the circumstances of life. From the standpoint of Soul Solitude, Spiritual Acceptance can be an even more profoundly powerful tool.

From a spiritual perspective,
"EVERYTHING IS AS IT MUST BE NOW."

Accepting that premise as valid is extremely difficult for many people. If everything is as it must be, there is no reason or need for "Shame, Blame, Judge and Justify." Acceptance is an incredibly effective "script-busting" technique.

That is why we can expect most people to initially reject this powerful spiritual tool. If everything is as it must be, then there is no payoff for being a victim or engaging in another "Poor Me Drama." Our scripts expect to be the only "truth" and tolerate no competition. If we accept the truth that everything is the way it must be, all other "truths" (scripts) slide into irrelevance.

Because everything is as it must be, we need to understand that is a truth about NOW, not the future. Once we see the necessity of NOW and are mindful of it, then we can use our "Seeing Through," "Thinking Through," and "Working Through" approach to choosing which set of possibilities to nurture. In the sense of Spiritual Acceptance, the past determines the

NOW, and we determine the FUTURE from this moment on.

Acceptance of the past and the "Nature of Things" allows us to be present to this particular NOW. While understandable, rejection of the necessity of the past forces us to continue living outside of the present, where Drama rules our lives. With Acceptance, we can live in the NOW. Without Acceptance, there is no NOW, just an endless succession of regrets, fears and frustrations as life slips through our fingers. We cannot live in the future or the past—so if we shut ourselves out of our NOW, we have effectively shut ourselves out of our own lives.

Acceptance is the key that unlocks that door. If we wish to quit being tourists in our own lives, we must continually repeat to ourselves while sitting silently:

EVERYTHING IS AS IT MUST BE NOW.
I AM AT PEACE.

Acceptance does not mean condoning or justifying abuse or trauma we may have experienced in the past. Acceptance allows us to contextualize our experience and provides meaning to the pain we have experienced in our journey. That we endured hardships and brutality are facts that must be confronted, but they are not Dramas that we must repeat over and over. Acceptance of the facts, despite whether or not they "should" have occurred, allows us to live fully in all the Arenas of our lives. Because of the difficulty many people experience with this important Central Spiritual Principle, we will need to explore several areas of concern.

Acceptance of the past is not the same as "forgiveness." Alice Miller, in her brilliant book, *The Drama of The Gifted Child*, cautions against premature forgiveness. Her contention is that forgiving too quickly or too easily can short-circuit important psychic processes and retard healing. That is one of the reasons Soul Solitude does not address the issue of "forgiveness." We deal with that more fully in our Improvisational Life Seminar. For now, within the context of Soul Solitude, Acceptance is mandatory, forgiveness is optional.

Later in the book, we will discuss the nature of our purpose in life. In regard to Acceptance, it is important to state that Soul Solitude is permeated by the belief that, for each of us, life has meaning and purpose. Because of that, our journey is both unfolding and preparing us for that purpose. While many of the things that we, and others, experience may be unjust, those experiences are necessary to achieving or fulfilling our purpose. The following is a story about what we call "unjust necessity."

The Old Man and the Butterfly

Once upon a time in a land far, far away. There was a wonderful old man who loved everything. Animals, spiders, insects . . .

One day, while walking through the woods, the nice old man found a cocoon.

Feeling lonely, he decided to take the cocoon home to watch its beautiful transformation from a funny little wispy shell to a beautiful butterfly.

He gently placed the cocoon on his kitchen table, and watched over it for days

Suddenly on the seventh day, the cocoon started to move. It moved frantically! The old man felt sorry for the little butterfly inside the cocoon. He watched it struggle and struggle and struggle!

Finally, the old man, feeling so sorry for the cocooned butterfly, rushed to its aid with a surgical scalpel and gently slit the cocoon so the butterfly could emerge.

Just one slice was all it took, and the butterfly broke free from its cocoon only to wilt over in a completely motionless state.

The old man did not know what to think. Had he accidentally killed the little butterfly? No, it's still moving a little bit! Maybe it's sick?

He was dumbfounded, and quite perplexed! "What should I do?" he said. He felt so sorry for the little creature that he decided the best thing he could do for the butterfly was to place it gently back into its cocoon.

He did so, and placed a drop of honey on it to seal the cocoon, leaving the butterfly to nestle in its natural state.

The next day he noticed that the cocoon was moving again. "Wow!" he said. It moved and moved and struggled and struggled. Finally the butterfly broke free from its cocoon and stretched its wings out far and wide. Its beautiful wings were filled with wonderful colors! It looked around and took off! It's flying! It's so beautiful! The old man was jumping with joy!

That wonderful butterfly did just that. It flew and flew till it was almost out of the old man's sight. "What a joy!" he exclaimed.

But then he started to think, "What did I do wrong by trying to help that beautiful little butterfly out at first?"

The old man went into town, found the library and read every book he could on butterflies and cocoons.

Finally the answer appeared. The butterfly has to struggle and struggle while inside the cocoon. That's how it gets its strength. That's just what they are designed to overcome in order to be strong and beautiful.

Needless to say, the old man was shocked, saddened and somewhat relieved.

Now he knows the reason why they do what they do. It was only his perception that made it appear that the butterfly was having a hard time. From then on, the old man knew that loving something sometimes means to pray for it and cheer it on!

He realized that God was wonderful, and that sometimes appearances aren't what they seem to be—that we all are beautiful butterflies, even though we have our apparent struggles in life.

(as found at www.stories.com, with thanks.)

Part of our journey is to accept that there are things that are normal, natural and necessary—things which may be very difficult on our Ego. But, like that butterfly, we may emerge from the struggle into the fullness and freedom of the person we were created to be. Other aspects of life that we need to accept might include:

1. Uncertainty
2. Imperfection
3. Powerlessness
4. Vulnerability
5. Responsibility (Appropriate/Un-inflated)

Uncertainty is unwelcome for most people, yet, in the sense of Soul Solitude, it is a primary part of the Way of Wonder.

Interestingly, an important part of quantum mechanics is what is called the *Heisenberg Uncertainty Principle.* This principle states that one can never know all the information about a particle. Either you know it's direction but not location, or you know it's location but not direction. This is true for life as well. Many people know where they are headed, but not where (or who) they are. Others know where or who they are but cannot tell you the direction of their life.

Within the context of Soul Solitude, mystery is the underlying nature of reality. We only think we know something, but we really don't. If we can accept that, then we can use our energy to deal with that reality. If we cannot accept mystery, we are going to spend all of our energy trying to escape it.

Perfection is a powerful script that many people are involved with, and usually don't know it. The language they use is normally about "high standards" and such. However, it is much more insidious than that. Soul Solitude is so simple, you cannot do it perfectly—you just do it. Accepting that we are imperfect allows us to break down all the shaming loops that taunt and torment us. We are perfectly human, which is to say, enormously imperfect. Accepting our imperfection is accepting our humanity.

Powerlessness and Vulnerability are really part of the same acceptance coin. Accepting that we have control over nothing is very liberating, but very threatening, because it leaves us vulnerable to all the vagaries and whims of the nature of things. We cannot be secure, unless we're powerful. So, if we have no control, we can be neither powerful or secure. Acceptance allows us to function freely with neither control or security.

Some people feel that they are responsible for virtually everything; others feel they are responsible for virtually nothing. Both are exaggerated positions. Acceptance, in the truest sense, is recognizing and accepting responsibility for those things for which we actually are responsible, such as: our words, our actions, our prejudices, our choices and our beliefs. Part of the sitting in silence allows us to actually consider what appropriate responsibility for our lives might include, without all the Drama and Expectations of Others. Once we know and accept responsibility appropriately, perhaps we can undertake appropriate actions to live up to our choices and the consequences of our words and actions. Once again, as we sit in the still sacred silence of Soul Solitude, we can say:

EVERYTHING IS AS IT MUST BE NOW.
I AM AT PEACE.

GRATITUDE

While Acceptance will be very difficult, Gratitude may be even more so. For most people, Gratitude is a ritual thing. We say thank you because somebody did something nice for us or gave us a gift. It's easy to say thank you for things we actually appreciate, but much more difficult to say thank you for things which do not seem like blessings at the time.

In her book, *The Hiding Place*, Corrie Ten Boom tells the story of her captivity, along with her sister, in a Nazi concentration camp during World War II. Their crime had been assisting Jews in escaping from the net of doom that was cast over them in Europe. The book is often more about the faith of her sister than that of the author. Nevertheless, it is an amazing testimony of hope amidst the incredible darkness of that horror.

One of the stories Corrie tells is of her sister insisting that they give thanks at the end of each day for all the "blessings" God had provided them that day. One of the horrible pestilences that afflicted them in their barracks were enormous swarms of gnats that flew in such thick clouds the guards would not even enter their barracks. Though horrified at the thought, Corrie's sister convinced her they should give thanks for the insects as well, which she reluctantly did. This went on for quite some time.

Interestingly, in spite of the rules of the prison, over time, the women of that barracks were able to gather in prayer and participate in the recounting of scripture stories each night, without fear of discovery by the guards. Their prison was guarded by the gossamer wings of a host of tiny little angels, whom even the sadistic guards would not challenge. While unwelcome in the beginning, the presence of those insects made life more bearable in those seemingly unbearable circumstances. Was gratitude an appropriate response?

In the movie, *Joe Vs. The Volcano*, Tom Hanks portrays a man who has nothing to live for, in search of himself. One of the scenes has him adrift on the ocean, dying of thirst. Suddenly the moon emerges, appearing in giant relief against the starry sky, and fills the entire ocean with light. On wobbly knees, Tom Hanks arises, and in dry-throated croaky tones says, "Oh God, whose name I do not know, thank you for my life." He then tumbles into unconsciousness. That moment of profound gratitude was Soul Solitude.

The experience of gratitude can be particularly painful for people who feel they have nothing to be grateful for. People who have been victimized, abused or traumatized will have great difficulty in framing that experience with gratitude. Like the sisters in the concentration camp, saying thanks for horror is at best unthinkable, at worst unconscionable.

We have encountered many people in life-threatening situations who began to see the blessings in their circumstance.

> Many times breakdowns provide the
> opportunity for breakthroughs which would
> be possible in no other way.

Those who cannot feel gratitude have a very different experience of life than those who can. We know it is almost impossible, but gratitude is necessary for dealing with the other Central Spiritual Principles that follow.

In the context of Soul Solitude, we feel it is important to express gratitude for:

Gifts
Mystery
History

Many blessings and gifts of our lives are not fully appreciated until we no longer have them. From that position of loss, the broken ego allows us to finally know what such gifts meant to us. Singers and athletes who can no longer perform so lament the loss that they can lose their sense of direction in life. Because they did not learn to be grateful then, they also cannot learn to be grateful NOW. Loss can be a tremendous, but harsh, teacher of gratitude. Sometimes, the lessons go unheeded.

A powerful mythic rendering of this truth is the tale of Orpheus.

> On the day that Orpheus and Eurydice were married, their wedding was marred by a terrible accident. After the nuptials, while Eurydice was walking in the fields with her attendants, she stepped on a snake and was bitten on the foot. Collapsing, she died shortly from the venom that coursed through her veins. Distraught, there was nothing that Orpheus could do to save his beloved bride. Undeterred by such a small matter as death, Orpheus undertook a journey to the underworld, singing his way through the obstacles set before him to bar his path. Upon reaching the underworld, Orpheus began singing for Queen Persephone and beseeching her to allow Eurydice to leave with him—since Eurydice would be returning soon enough, after leading a normal life.
>
> Apparently, Orpheus was such a gifted singer and musician that the affairs of the underworld virtually came to a halt in order for the Shades to hear his song. His request was granted, on the condition that Eurydice would return to Hades immediately if Orpheus so much as looked over his shoulder to see if she was there. Making their way to the surface they had almost arrived at safety, when for some reason, Orpheus looked back. Immediately, Eurydice began drifting back along the path on which they had struggled. Orpheus was unable to maintain the hold he had on his bride who slipped away into the abyss. As Ovid puts it, "And she dying again made no complaint, for what complaint had she but that she was loved?"

What was lacking for Orpheus is the sense of gratitude for all that he experienced. Afterward, he was so distraught that he basically threw his life away.

How can we be grateful when we lose a loved one? Unlike Orpheus, our gifts are no match for the mystery of death and loss. Yet, the only way through grief is through it. There are no shortcuts or easy roads. As we become grateful for the gift and mystery of those we love in our lives, both while they are alive and after they pass from us, we discover that there is so much more to be grateful about—that they were in our lives, at all!

Which brings us to the gift and mystery of our own lives. Are we grateful only if the circumstances of our lives are what they were "supposed" to be? Isn't the fact that we exist enough? Isn't the fact that we are loved enough? Isn't the fact that we participate in a complex and dynamic world filled with mystery and wonder enough? When will our cup be full enough to be grateful? Grateful to whom or what?

Finally, gratitude for our history is a very perplexing phenomena. In his book, *Man's Search for Meaning*, Viktor Frankl suggests that, even in the most depraved situation, there were those who transcended their circumstances and became beacons of hope for others. Frankl himself is one such individual. His words have enlightened countless numbers of people—yet such a book would never have been written had he and others not endured the sufferings of the concentration camp. How could we ever know that there is light in the darkest places that the soul can descend to? Should we be grateful for his history? We ponder such things most effectively in Soul Solitude.

EVERYTHING IS AS IT MUST BE NOW.
I AM AT PEACE.

TRUST

*P*erhaps one of the most demanding and dangerous principles of anyone's spiritual journey is Trust. Many people think of trust as an economic commodity that can be earned or offered as a reward. The reality is that Trust is a gift. No one deserves it, no one is owed Trust. Trust is fairly dichotomous in that you either give it or you don't. You cannot trust a little or a lot, you either trust or you do not. To trust a little is to not trust.

The first area of trust we need to consider is the ability to trust ourselves. We need to trust that we have what it takes to deal with life as it unfolds. If we lack this basic level of trust, we are constantly living in fear that catastrophe is just around the corner and we will not be able to recover. We are always waiting for that proverbial "other shoe" to drop. Many people doubt their ability to deal with the pain, difficulty and complexity of life, so they seek to avoid being exposed to these normal and natural, though unwanted, aspects of life. Within such attempts to avoid exposure is the seedbed of Drama and escape.

The Ego trusts no one, not even itself. Since we cannot give gifts we do not possess, the Ego can neither give nor receive trust. People who have been abused or traumatized find trusting others to be extremely difficult. So what is trust?

The Merriam-Webster Online Dictionary defines trust as:

> 1 a: *assured reliance on the character, ability, strength, or truth of someone or something; b: one in which confidence is placed*
>
> 2 a: *dependence on something future or contingent :* HOPE; b: *reliance on future payment for property (as merchandise) delivered :* CREDIT *<bought furniture on trust>*
>
> 3 a: *a property interest held by one person for the benefit of another; b: a combination of firms or corporations formed by a legal agreement; especially : one that reduces or threatens to reduce competition*
>
> 4 archaic : TRUSTWORTHINESS
>
> 5 a (1): *a charge or duty imposed in faith or confidence or as a condition of some relationship* (2) : *something committed or entrusted to one to be used or cared for in the interest of another; b: responsible charge or office; c:* CARE, CUSTODY *<the child committed to her trust>*
> - in trust : *in the care or possession of a trustee*

Other dictionaries define the word similarly. Our approach is much simpler. We define trust as a matter of "mattering." If I matter to myself, then I can trust

that my life has meaning and significance. Because
my life has meaning and significance, then I can trust
that I have what it takes to realize that meaning and
significance of my life. I can trust the source of the
meaning and significance of my life, because I matter
to that source, whatever we term that entity or system.
Because I matter to the source, I can trust the basic
premise of the Central Spiritual Principles:

EVERYTHING IS AS IT MUST BE NOW.
I AM AT PEACE.

If I can trust this to be true, then I have what it takes
to deal with everything that unfolds in my life. I can
trust that I will experience things that will assist my
Soul in learning and growing, and I can trust that such
experiences may be extremely difficult for my Ego. I
can trust that people will abandon, betray or destroy
me. But, I can trust that I have what it takes to deal
with such matters. I can trust others, knowing that
they are capable of causing me pain and difficulty. But
I can trust that I have what it takes to deal with such
matters.

I have every reason and every right to trust no one.
But if I fail to trust the Source, myself or others,
my alternative is to live in fear and trembling. Even
though my life will end in death, I need to trust
that even that mystery is part of the larger mystery
which engulfs me. Trust is impossible, but absolutely
necessary.

Within the context of Soul Solitude, we learn to trust:

- Who We Are
- Where We Are
- Where We're Going

Trust is a choice we make and a gift we give. While it may never come easily, until we learn to trust, life is very difficult. Once we learn this skill, finally, we can trust:

EVERYTHING IS AS IT MUST BE NOW.
I AM AT PEACE.

SURRENDER

*L*etting go sounds so easy, yet as many can attest, the reality is quite different. Why would we hang on to scripts that are toxic or control us? Why would we hang on to Drama that enslaves and limits us? Why would we continue to identify with our Circumstances or the Expectations of Others? Why would we hold on when the price continues to rise and the benefits continue to diminish? Hanging on is so difficult while letting go is so easy—yet we persist in hanging on to outdated modes of being in the world. Why is that?

Every life is filled with possibilities and limitations. While we are not the circumstances of our lives, within those circumstances are the teachings and teachers we need for our lives to continue toward our purpose. While we are not *defined by* the circumstances of our lives, we are constrained and challenged by those circumstances. They are there for us to be challenged to learn and grow. Within the circumstances of our lives, we experience change and upheaval that helps us to know more clearly who we are. Sometimes, as we explored earlier, we are faced with choices that we would rather not make. All of this is painfully complex and difficult.

Some of our circumstances we can change, others we cannot. All of the circumstances of our lives *will* change, whether we wish it or not. When we cannot change the circumstances, do we continue to struggle, or do we surrender peacefully? There is no script for such choices, so what is the appropriate response to seemingly arbitrary reality?

One observation we have made is that people cling to their mythologies of the past long after reality changes. The most obvious example of this is the "phantom limb pain" that amputees experience long after the limb has been removed. Many people cling to the hope that a loved one will be found alive, long after any hope of rescue or discovery has elapsed. Many people who have been fired or laid off from a job continue to awake, ready to go to work—and sometimes take considerable time to recover from the disbelief they do not work there any more. The same can be said for marriages and other losses.

Ultimately, we may be confronted with voluntarily surrendering our life. In a sense, we are all preparing for that final surrender. Some go peacefully, some do not. Some will cling tenaciously to life, some will let go without a struggle. Context always determines the appropriateness of any response. Most of us would prefer to die in our sleep and not have to make this choice, while others hope to be conscious until the very end. Surrendering to mystery is an immense spiritual journey that awaits each of us. Perhaps our unknown end can help shape that journey even now. Perhaps we can surrender to the knowledge and mystery:

EVERYTHING IS AS IT MUST BE NOW.
I AM AT PEACE.

So, these are the essential pillars of Soul Solitude: Mindfulness and Presence, Acceptance, Gratitude, Trust and Surrender. These are simple principles to learn, but not easy to practice. The interesting thing about these principles is that there are no masters or experts in them—all are equal. One either knows them or does not; one either practices them or does not. Perfection is not required. There is no right or wrong way to apply these principles, there is only the application or avoidance. The sequence does not matter. Whether you apply some or all really does not matter, because they each lead to the other.

Once you learn the principles, no one can really teach you more about them—they are dependent upon your experience. From this moment on, there is no one more "qualified" than you are. We offer Improvisational Life Seminars to enrich and expand each other's reflection upon them, but we also learn a great deal from those who attend. Of course, there is more to our seminars than the principles, but we are all students of this incredible mystery. We teach and learn together. So, from this moment on, we invite you to walk in mystery and dance in wonder.

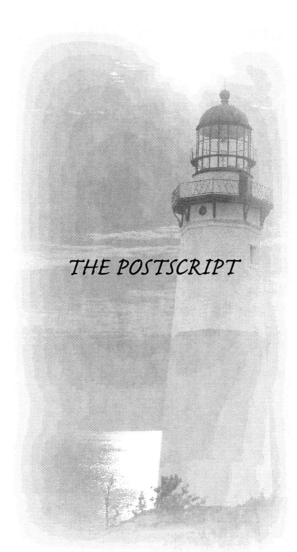

THE POSTSCRIPT

*A*t one level, spirituality is a poetic way of expressing certain types and qualities of experience. Such experiences may best be discussed in the language of metaphor and symbols. Within the poetic context of spirituality, and specifically Soul Solitude, we discuss the metaphors of:

- Landscape (Themescape)
- Pathway
- Journey
- Destination
- Traveler

Whatever path one may be on, whatever type of journey or whatever destination one may be headed for, we all travel through the same landscape. Soul Solitude is a way of describing and dealing with the demands of that overall spiritual landscape for each traveler, destination, journey and pathway. We feel that the practice of Soul Solitude can enrich the spiritual journey by attending to those matters of pain, difficulty and complexity that each person experiences as a consequence of that landscape.

DRAMA VS DHARMA

*I*n our earlier discussion, we explored at some length the idea of Drama in our life. One final area to explore is to contrast Drama with Dharma. Dharma is a Sanskrit word that involves the idea of purpose. Actually, Dharma is destiny without the Drama.

Deepak Chopra states that there are three aspects of Dharma to consider:

> *Life is a spiritual journey, our time is limited and our life is temporary.*
>
> *We each possess certain gifts we are expected to utilize as we make our way through life.*
>
> *We are created for service, with the expectation that our journey is not exclusively about ourselves.*

The best way to describe Dharma from the perspective of Soul Solitude is to use a traffic analogy.

A green car and a pink car are on the road headed for the same destination. The green car accelerates and changes lanes often, trying to get ahead of the pink car. All this maneuvering about is in the vain hope that there will be some magic break in the heavy traffic that will allow arriving at the destination first, and hopefully significantly earlier, than the pink car. Meanwhile, the pink car calmly follows the cars ahead of it—no drama, no rush, not endangering self or others—just peacefully making the journey.

Chances are that both cars will arrive at the destination at nearly the same time, but the quality of the journey will be significantly different. While the one driver spent all his attention and energy trying to manipulate the circumstances, the other driver quietly listened to music and enjoyed the sky and sunshine and flowers along the way. The first is Drama, the second is Dharma.

Dharma is the idea that each life has purpose and meaning, and we will achieve that purpose with or without the drama. Acceptance, gratitude, trust and surrender are ways of allowing Dharma to lead us through the pain, difficulty and complexity that we are normally bound to experience. By following Dharma, there is the possibility that we will experience profound joy in our journey. With Drama, there is little chance of that.

As we engage in the process of Soul Solitude, we can become mindful of the differences of the two approaches to life. We can mindfully choose Dharma or Drama, it's up to each of us. Such distinctions will become increasingly important as we engage more fully in Soul Solitude.

As we mentioned earlier, each of us is part of a number of systems in each of the Arenas of Life. The nature of systems is that they tend to equilibrium as their preferred state of being. When equilibrium is disturbed, each system makes changes in order to restore the previous state of equilibrium. If such a return is impossible, the system will attempt to establish a new state of equilibrium.

How this comes into play with Soul Solitude is that, as we begin to matter, the systems of which we are part will begin to change and lose their valued equilibrium. If a system was entirely based upon the premise that you don't matter, by mattering to yourself you are going to create significant disturbance in that system. Perhaps the entire system will break down, and change will necessarily need to occur.

This can be very traumatic. Do not be dismayed. Trauma is a tool of drama. Breakdown often needs to occur in order for a breakthrough to take place. Others wanting to maintain the equilibrium will predict all sorts of catastrophes for you if you do not return to your previous pattern. You will be considered selfish, ungrateful, disrespectful and many other terms designed to shame you or force you to reconsider your change and return to the fold. Transformation is rarely appreciated, approved of or supported. The choice is to return to "not mattering" or to go forth, trusting the path of Dharma and the Way of Wonder.

IMPROVISATIONAL LIFE

*T*his way of being in the world is what we call "Improvisational Life," because it does not have a prearranged script for how to be that way. We have seminars that explore in depth what such "Walking In Mystery and Dancing In Wonder" is all about. The following are a few highlights from that.

Whether we intend it that way or not, Soul Solitude leads to an Improvisational Life. As we begin to experience the fullness of our life—the freedom of our life, mindfulness and consciousness, and ultimately profound joy—people will begin to experience us very differently. You will begin to notice people saying,

> *"There's something different about you. I can't tell what it is, but you have changed."*

As you begin to know who you are, they won't. People will begin to relate to you in extraordinarily different ways.

This is where the Dharmic concept of gifts enters the picture. The actual gifts that we have been given are not always the gifts our Ego wishes to acknowledge. As Emerson is purported to have said,

> *To laugh often and much; to win the respect of intelligent people and the affection of children, to earn the appreciation of honest critics and endure the betrayal of false friends; to appreciate beauty, to find the best in others; to leave the world a bit better, whether by a healthy child, a garden patch or a redeemed social condition; to know even one life has breathed easier because you have lived. This is to have succeeded.*

Such gifts are rarely counted among the Ego's treasures. These are Soul gifts that offer success and wealth beyond measure, but are rarely seen on a balance sheet or a resumé. What are the gifts that your soul invites you to share with the world? Perhaps, in the sacred silence of Soul Solitude, you might consider such a question.

As we consider our gifts, the final area of Dharma is service to the world. Not everyone is called to the Peace Corps or other obvious ways of serving others. Providing meaningful employment to people with limited opportunities is one way we have found to serve.

One very touching story is about a retired kindergarten teacher in Minnesota, who worked tirelessly day after day in her local church to serve people who had lost their homes to devastating floods in 2007. The interesting thing about her was that she, too, had lost her home to the same flood, but rather than focusing on her problems, she decided it was better to reach out to others. Some might consider that denial. We consider it Dharma.

No one can really predict how or when to serve. Most of the time the need emerges as life unfolds.

A favorite imaginal story is about a farmer, in a Roman Colony in the early first century.

The land was difficult to work, the water scarce and the climate dry. Each day he would get up wondering if there was a greater purpose in his life than the dull drudgery of subsistence farming. He felt that his life had considerably more meaning than his circumstances, but he had no idea what that could possibly be. One day he got up and started planting for the next season's crop, paying little attention to the passerby on the nearby road. He noticed the man, waved hello and continued with his chore. The passerby watched for a while and then continued on his own way, talking with those who were with him.

While the farmer was sowing seeds, there were the usual problems with the birds, the rocks and the dry soil. The farmer paid little attention to these nuisances. That night, he said prayers and went to sleep, still wondering about the meaning of his existence.

Unbeknown to the farmer, while standing at the road, the passerby had looked deeply into the details of the farmer's struggle to get his field to grow. The passerby noticed that some of the seed fell on rocky ground and would never take root. Other seeds fell where the birds or the wind would scatter the seeds, and they too would never bear fruit. Of course, there were always the problems with the weeds. But some of those seeds fell on good ground and would yield a successful crop. Through the eyes and words of that passerby, the spiritual journeys of millions of people

*have been nourished for thousands of years by that simple
farmer.*

The farmer was unaware that he was living a parable,
a profound message for others. Perhaps that farmer
never knew the power of Dharma, but many have
known the power of that parable. Who is to say how
we actually serve the world?

By our very being in the world, each of us may be
serving in some unimagined way. Our Ego may not
appreciate such service, for it cannot profit from such
things. The Ego is always looking for compensation—
afraid of missing out or being taken advantage of. In
today's world, such a farmer would insist on royalties
or some form of payment for being used in such an
egregious way. Yet, we are convinced that such service
continues to occur in our world.

THE LIGHT OF SOUL SOLITUDE

*A*s we come to the end of our exploration of Soul Solitude, we consider that farmer, the unknown beacon of hope and meaning for nearly two thousand years. We think of him like a lighthouse—a still, steadfast beacon shining with the light of Soul Solitude against the night and the elements. Against the tides that incessantly surge against it, the lighthouse stands. Not to control or do mighty things, the task of the lighthouse is to be true to its nature, to stand in purposeful silence and shining splendor. The inner light projected outward to resist the drama of the sea and elements that rush against the rocks and to signal the ships that depend on the lighthouse being steadfast and constant.

Dharma is not drama, and the lighthouse is filled with Dharma. Such steadfast serenity is a powerful testimony to the strength and purpose of Soul Solitude.

As you engage is Soul Solitude, you too will become a lighthouse for others. As they scurry about, dancing to the Expectations of Others, or Addicted to Drama, you may help them see that they DO matter. They are not their scripts nor their circumstances. Like you, they will no longer need to shame, blame, judge and justify. They too can find fullness, freedom, mindfulness and joy in Soul Solitude. Because of your steadfast serenity, they too may be able to walk in mystery and dance in wonder.

Acceptance, Gratitude, Trust, Surrender
Soul Centering Principles that engender
All I need to remember
Who I Am.

APPENDICES

APPENDIX ONE:
CORE VALUES PROFILE™

In the context of Soul Solitude, one of the very most important aspects of consciousness is the central question of "Who Am I?" Some elements of that answer are going to be flexible and change over time, while others are going to remain fairly stable throughout our lifetime. One of the ways we can learn more about ourselves is through the use of an instrument called the Core Values Profile.

The Core Values Profile helps us develop a picture of the deepest aspects of our being, our "Core Values." These are different than what we call "Rational Values," such as family, health, God and so forth. The Core Values Profile helps us understand our deep, intrinsic values that we were born with, our instinctual values. These are the foundation upon which the core of our being is built.

The Core Values Profile was developed within a business setting, so its entire orientation is about practical application. Other instruments were developed in psychological centers or clinical settings, usually with people outside of their normal surroundings. The Core Values Profile is not setting-specific, so it is useful in any situation. The Core Values Profile does not measure behavior, intelligence or aptitude. It is totally different than other instruments.

With the information generated by the Core Values Profile, we can know more clearly the types of things that are going to be attractive to us and those things which we may prefer to avoid. It allows us to gather information about ourselves in a very non-threatening and informative way. Once you understand this information, you can use it to help in your business life, your relational life and even your spiritual life.

Since the Core Values Profile is an online instrument, it is very quick and easy to take. The information is generated promptly and available over the internet. Because of the amazing stability of our core values, the information changes little over time. So, there is no need to take the Core Values Profile very often. As a matter of fact, it is not recommended to take more often than every three or four years. You will be amazed at the depth and accuracy of this instrument.

To take the Core Values Profile, go on line to http://www.CoreValuesProfile.com. We know that you will find this information of particular interest because of your interest in Soul Solitude.

APPENDIX TWO:
DHARMIC THEMESCAPE

(An Introduction)

We have used this paradigm in our work for a number of years to help people understand and reconcile some of the contradictions they encounter in their experience of various religious and spiritual systems. This paradigm has proven useful in exploring and explaining the spiritual journey and landscape to people, and has proven helpful in various times and places in the decision-making process of day-to-day living. It is a synthesis that provides a useful structure for dealing with religious and other "wisdom systems."

Many wisdom systems suggest that life is some version or combination of:

Painful
Difficult
Complicated.

Life can be painful because of the difficulties and complexities we encounter on our journey. Life is all too brief, health is fragile, relationships come and go and people are seemingly always in transition and encountering losses of all sorts. We are filled with uncertainty, imperfections, and countless vulnerabilities. Ultimately, we are nearly powerless to change or impact our lives, the lives of those we love, or the world, very much.

Life can be difficult because of the pain and complexities we encounter. Many people are searching for something: some search for meaning, some for impact and some are searching for specific types of experience. What is the purpose of life? Are we here to create or destroy, lead or follow, and so many other choices? We are burdened by the blessings and joys of our lives, our personal gifts and ultimately the mystery of it all. Through life's difficulties, our identities are forged, our secrets and darkness are exposed and our destinies revealed.

Life can be complex because of the pains and difficulties we encounter. There are so many constraints that life imposes, so many challenges, so many choices which we are insufficiently prepared to make. We're often limited by our perceptions and must settle for dealing in a world of incomplete approximations that are of dubious validity. We are always dealing with the ramifications of our fears, beliefs and desires and are constantly confronted with the reality of death, change and uncertainty.

That doesn't mean that every moment of every day in human experience can be summed up as painful, difficult or complicated, but, on the whole, that seems to be a pretty accurate expression of the human journey. Whether or not we choose to accept the choices life presents to us, there are almost always consequences to the "external" circumstances of our life, as well as consequences within our own personal "inner" experience. The Dharmic Themescape is an attempt to describe some of the dynamics that occur in the never-ending process of choosing and living.

Life As A Journey

Since the early years of the twentieth century, when Albert Einstein articulated his theories of relativity, we have had a new vocabulary to express the nature of reality. With the formula $E=MC^2$, we know that even matter is fundamentally energy, and all energy is in "flow." With the "Big Bang," when the flow of energy and "space/time" began, so did our universe. Within that flow of energy and time, there were some "fluctuations" in the flow, that we call *matter*. Those fluctuations in the flow of time and energy remained anonymous until human beings emerged, who were able to interpret those fluctuations and translate them into meaningful information: trees, rocks, stars and so forth.

In the most basic sense, then, the universe consists of the flow of time, energy and information.

In the more mundane context of human living, our lives are about keeping track of fluctuations in the flow of time and energy. Early in our evolution, people noticed that there were cyclic events in the phenomenal world (cycles of the sun, the moon, the stars, flooding etc.) that helped to differentiate aspects of the flow of experience. In order to help remember the sequence of events in life, humans began to tell stories. Undifferentiated experience could be disorienting to early humans, and this can be true in our own lives as well.

At some point in our evolution, people began thinking of their lives as a "journey" proceeding from birth to death and even beyond. In this context, our lives are a story, in which we fill in the details as we go. But as in any story, there are certain basic questions that seem to occur in nearly everyone's life:

- Who am I? (Identity)
- Where do I come from? (Origins)
- Where am I going? (Destiny)

So, at the heart of the Dharmic Themescape is the journey of our life which endeavors to discover and answer those basic questions.

Figure 2 (see page 93) is a graphic representation and summary of this entire discussion. It might be helpful to examine it first and then keep it handy for reference as we continue.

Outward Dimension of Our Journey

The great psychoanalyst, Carl Jung, described one of the fundamental processes of being human as the process of *Individuation*, where we separate from our parents and home of origin to become autonomous human beings. On the outward journey, through a variety of processes, we more or less leave our home of origin and seek our fortunes in the world. Sometimes, this process of leaving home is voluntary, and sometimes not. In any event, there's normally a tension that arises, namely the desire to return home. A great deal of our life is dealing with the dynamics of separation and reconciliation with parents and with our past selves. In a certain sense, one could assert that the Garden of Eden story could be addressing many of these themes.

Inward Dimension of Our Journey

As we more fully engage the outer world, often people become alienated from their inner selves.

Perhaps, as we become more successful at achieving independence, we wind up ignoring what's going on inside us, until at some point we begin to experience inner turmoil. Individuation has to occur on both the inner and outer dimensions of our lives.

A fairly common example of this tension might be the man who marries and begins to raise his own family (outward individuation) but continues to dote over his mother, because he has not fully separated from her within his own inner being. This inner "letting go" can be, in many ways, far more difficult than the outward process. Interestingly, one of the contradictions of life occurs after we have individuated—where at some point, in order to achieve wholeness, the parts that are separated must also be reunified.

So, we can see that successful individuation/separation and reconciliation/unification can lead to both liberation and empowerment, which allows us to function more effectively in both the inner and outer dimensions of life. On the other hand, if this process is handled poorly, we can be dealing with attachment and dependence problems all our lives—on either or both the external and internal levels.

Expectations Of Life

Depending on how we've handled the individuation/ unification issues of growth, we can form certain habitual patterns of expectation that shape the ways we respond to life. For the purposes of our discussion here, we will consider these issues as if they were fully manifested one way or the other. In most people's life, these things are handled imperfectly and are characterized by different aspects of healthy and unhealthy patterns. For this discussion, we'll exaggerate both sides a little.

Outward Expectations of Life

Poor individuation means that often we will have problems dealing with the pain, complexity and difficulties of life. These patterns are characterized by a desire and need for immunity, compensation or escape. (See Fig. 2).

Expectations of Immunity: characterized by the feeling that for some reason, particular negative circumstances of life shouldn't be happening to us. "Why is this happening to me?" is the frequently asked question about the underlying expectation that somehow I should be immune to any particular set of experiences of life. "I don't deserve this" or "It just isn't fair" are commonly heard laments characterizing this expectation. When we're rational, we realize that life isn't fair and what we deserve has nothing to do with what happens in life. However, many of us feel that unwanted reality only visits other people, not us. When it inevitably intrudes in our lives, we go into psychic shock. We often refer to this as "magical" thinking.

Expectations of Compensation: when unwanted reality confronts us, the expectation can arise that somebody's going to "pay for this" experience. "Somebody has to be responsible for what I'm going through!" This is really a deflection mechanism that diverts our attention from what we're actually going through, and sets up a chain of events that can lead to compulsions such as revenge or vindictiveness. When all is said and done, there is no sufficient compensation for the pain, difficulty and complexity of what we experience. So we begin to compensate by indulging ourselves in ways designed to make us feel better. This is rarely a good long-term strategy.

Expectation of Escape: As a result of the other expectations, ultimately this one is under our control and eventually leads further into dependence and darkness. Whether drugs, alcohol or even suicide, there are a variety of self-destructive strategies we can employ to escape the pain of life. Often, by over-indulging in our compensation strategies, we begin the process of voluntary or involuntary escape that can often be dangerous and trigger additional unwanted reality. So, of course, the cycle begins again.

Proper individuation/reconciliation offers some clear alternatives. While life is no less painful, difficult or complicated for such people, they have a totally different set of expectations.

Expectation of Community: This is simply the sense that we are not alone in the things that we experience. Intense pain and loss can be very isolating, "No one knows what I am going through," is a legitimate feeling at such times. It can be very helpful when we open ourselves up to the experiences of others and know that, while our experience is unique, others have experienced similar situations. It is comforting to know that no one walks an easy road all the time.

Expectation of Consolation: Properly integrated people console and can be consoled by others when confronted with the pain and difficulties of life. Their experiences often help them to be more compassionate and empathetic to the pain and struggles of others. Time and again, we've known people who, though they were going through their own trauma in life, took the time to listen and console others who were experiencing pain.

Expectation of Engagement: These people are fully engaged in whatever life throws at them. If it's an illness, they study and learn all they can about it, join support groups and seek out others who have experienced similar difficulties. Even when confronted with mortal agony, they sometimes eschew pain medication so that they can be fully lucid up to their last breath. These people dance and enjoy life up until the very end. To be fully engaged with the pain, difficulties and complexities of life is to be fully alive.

Inward Experiences of Life

This area of experience is much more difficult to discuss. Rather than dichotomize the different elements as we did above, we're going to discuss them as transformational processes, a movement from attachment/dependence toward liberation and empowerment.

Perhaps the best description of the inner reality of dependence/attachment is one of darkness, diffusion and despair. The pain, difficulties and complications of life are so intense and exaggerated there seems to be no way out. Everything seems difficult and there is almost no energy to deal with anything. Options, if they exist, are very limited and mostly unappealing. In this state, options that would normally be unthinkable seem like workable solutions. In this state of affairs, the only option is to do nothing or seek help.

The journey away from the precipice of darkness is to move toward and become the light. The power of light (even the merest glimmer) is a powerful beacon of hope in this darkness. Our sense of identity becomes more coherent as we begin to get in touch

with parts of our inner selves from which we've been
cut off for seemingly endless ages. That which felt
so burdensome and heavy becomes a joy to carry.
No logical explanation for this process exists that
we know of, but we do have experience with it. The
following poem is about such experience:

A GLIMMER IN THE DARKNESS
G. Charles Andersen

Now the shattered visions
> *And all my broken dreams*
> *And all the tears of bitterness*
> > *Overwhelm me like a flood,*
Or so it seems.

And yet,
Deep within my tortured soul
Some tiny, obstinate spark of hope
Holds off the darkness
> *From engulfing me.*

Undaunted, unyielding
Against the irresistible onrush of night
That tiny spark remains.
A fragile bastion
Of unconquerable power

Pitted against the merciless

> *Onslaught of terror and doubt,*

That vainly seeks to put out

> *The hidden promise*

Of the coming dawn.

THE BALANCE OF DIVERGENT PATHS

In the New Testament, Jesus talks about two divergent paths, the spiritual path he is advocating and the one that the religious leaders of his day offer. Within the context of the Themescape, these two divergent paths are called the "The Way of Will" and the "The Way of Wonder." The ways Jesus describes them is indicated often by the "You've heard it said . . . but I say to you…" sayings. A favorite outline for the Way of Wonder is the following:

> [25] *"Therefore I tell you, do not worry about your life, what you will eat (or drink), or about your body, what you will wear. Is not life more than food and the body more than clothing?*
>
> [26] *Look at the birds in the sky; they do not sow or reap, they gather nothing into barns, yet your heavenly Father feeds them. Are not you more important than they?*
>
> [27] *Can any of you by worrying add a single moment to your life-span?*
>
> [28] *Why are you anxious about clothes? Learn from the way the wild flowers grow. They do not work or spin.*
>
> [29] *But I tell you that not even Solomon in all his splendor was clothed like one of them.*

[30] *If God so clothes the grass of the field, which grows today and is thrown into the oven tomorrow, will he not much more provide for you, O you of little faith?*

[31] *So do not worry and say, "What are we to eat?" or "What are we to drink?" or "What are we to wear?"*
Matthew 6:25-34

THE WAY OF WONDER

Jesus, Buddha, and other spiritual teachers seem to be advocating a path that is different from the one that most of us are willing to venture upon. This is an ancient path that leads to Wisdom, Authenticity, Integrity and Humility. This is the path we read about in various stories and scriptures.

Regardless of our age, leaving the familiar and predictable behind must be a difficult and challenging decision. The qualities of Wisdom, Authenticity, Integrity and Humility are ones that we probably all would like to develop, but we want to develop them within the context of the more familiar territory offered by the Way of Will. After all, if you are on the Way of Wonder, how do you know if you are a success or not? One cannot undertake the Way of Wonder without a sense of liberation and empowerment, because there's little external support for such a choice.

The Way of Wonder requires us to lighten our load quite a bit. Most of the baggage of life is unnecessary. The primary issues of this path revolve around:

- Our sense of being
- Our sense of belonging
- Our sense of becoming

These are issues directly related to the primary journey issues of:

- Who am I?
- Where do I come from?
- Where am I going?

The Way of Wonder is not a forced march into the future. The only way of entering this path is by letting go, which many people find to be daunting. In order to follow the Way of Wonder, there is a counter-intuitive process involved. The dynamic at work here is the four-fold process of:

1. Acceptance
2. Gratitude
3. Trust
4. Surrender.

Interestingly, this four-fold process underlies much of the success of twelve-step programs. Without going into the applicability of the twelve steps, we can explore some of the basic aspects of this four fold process.

ACCEPTANCE

God is the author of reality—we might not like it but that doesn't change the fundamental nature of what we experience. So what are we supposed to accept?

Uncertainty: Even in the world of Physical Science, uncertainty rules. There is no way of knowing enough about causes or consequences or conditions to be truly certain about anything. Regardless, many people seek an unrealistic degree of predictability and remain frustrated by the mysteries of life. Acceptance of uncertainty allows us to spend our energies in more productive pursuits.

Imperfection: Nearly everyone pays lip service to being "imperfect," yet the quest for perfection is a hallmark of our culture. To be able to accept our limitations is the first step toward true liberation.

Powerlessness: We can't control the people and events around us, yet time and again we try. We go so far as to try to manipulate God (by prayers and sacrifices) in order to impact circumstances to turn out our way. The truth is simply that nearly everything is beyond our power to control. Even if we seem to have control, the uncertainties of life mentioned above are almost guaranteed to provide a range of unforeseen consequences, over which we have no control.

Vulnerability: There really is no poultice or panacea to protect us from the pain of life. Neither wealth nor power can protect us from change or unwanted reality. Wisdom seems to indicate that accepting vulnerability (without seeking or creating more) allows us the freedom to live more creatively.

Responsibility: (Appropriate/Un-inflated)

> Many people don't accept
> responsibility for their actions,
> while others burden themselves with
> responsibilities that are not truly
> theirs. Even though we're uncertain,
> powerless and vulnerable, we are
> responsible to ourselves and to
> others for the mistakes and injuries
> we cause as we journey through life.
> Even though we create unintended
> consequences, true integration
> requires us to accept appropriate
> responsibility for our words and
> actions.

Gratitude

Because of our limited perception, it's difficult to be grateful for things we don't want. In the context of the Dharmic Themescape, all that we experience has meaning and is necessary for our personal and collective growth.

So what are we to be grateful for? Probably anything we don't want as well as that which we do want. As Job so eloquently puts it:

"If we take happiness from God's hand, must we not take sorrow too?" Job 2:10

Among the things to be grateful for could be:

Blessings: (Burdens & Joys)

> Some blessings are easier to be
> grateful for than others. Developing

an attitude of gratitude is essential for a positive sense of well being.

Gifts: (Personal)

Many people demean their own gifts because they are not the gifts or talents they desire. Each person has particular capabilities, but some are not in touch with what their gifts truly are. Awareness and gratitude for our unique qualities is particularly important in the ongoing journey of life.

Mystery: (Sacred-Holy-Real)

Mystery surrounds us everywhere, but are we grateful for mystery in our lives? There are those whose lives are dedicated to eliminating and escaping from mystery, while others spend their lives trying to embrace it. What does it mean to be grateful for mystery, and how does it enrich our lives?

History:

Many people are filled with regrets and resentments from the past. Yet, as we look back we can see that the unwanted memories and events of our lives have shaped and defined us. Can we be truly grateful for our own being if we're not grateful for our history?

Trust

For many of us who grew up under difficult circumstances, trust can be a very difficult issue to deal with. We experience life very much like the Charles Schultz cartoon character, Charlie Brown. Time after time, Charlie Brown goes to kick the football from the hands of Lucy, only to flop after the ball has been withdrawn suddenly. Regardless of our experience, growth can only occur when we continue to trust, even in spite of our experience. Among the things we need to trust are:

Who We Are
Where We Are
Where We're Going

Surrender

The circumstances (including all our possibilities and limitations) of life are filled with an endless variety of Constraints, Challenges, Choices, Changes, and Complexities, whether or not we like it. Ultimately, we cannot control other people or circumstances. We can only surrender to reality and respond to it as best we can. For many, this seems somewhat fatalistic. However, there's great wisdom in not spending our energies pursuing impossible strategies. This is the attitude expressed in the serenity prayer:

God, grant me the serenity to accept the things

I cannot change...

Courage to change the things I can, and

Wisdom to know the difference.

Ultimately, the Way of Wonder leads to a life of compassion, creativity and contentment. However, the path is not certain, predictable or pain-free.

The Way of Will

The Way of Will is a far more alluring prospect to most people. It offers us the compelling temptations of power, perfection, security and superiority. "If you want to be successful, you must be on this path." However, this is the path of the well-known "rat race" of life. It's about getting ahead, doing more, having more and trying to keep what you've worked so hard to attain. It's a path that justifies whatever it takes to get where one is going or what one wants. Of course, there's the inevitable problem of achieving what you set out to accomplish, and finding that once you are there, it still is not enough, or is not all that it promised to be. So, inevitably the cycle must begin again.

Denial is a very helpful tool in this path of condemnation and compulsion. Control becomes more and more of an issue, as it becomes more and more elusive.

Final Ring of Awareness

As we explore the Dharmic Themescape (Fig. 2), we realize that it does not describe a linear journey, but more of a spiral path. Sometimes we focus on the inward experience, while at other times our outward encounters occupy or overwhelm us. Some aspects of our life reflect the Way of Wonder, while at other times we walk squarely through the Way of Will.

Surrounding the Themescape and forming the four outer quadrants are the elements of Magic, Mastery, Mindfulness and Mystery.

There are times and circumstances in our journey when we exhibit some form of "Magical Thinking" which, in psychological parlance, is called denial. The art of a magician is based upon illusions. To date, I am unaware of people with the power to actually manipulate matter in the ways they claim. Usually, they are able to fabricate an experience through deception and misdirection, which, because of our state of mind, we accept as "real." If one stops to analyze our culture, a great deal of marketing capitalizes on this aspect of Magical Thinking. If we get such and such a product (and only that particular brand of product), we will magically achieve something that's elusive but important to us. Rarely is there a genuine payoff for this process, but because of the pervasive nature (and the profit motive) we are continually bombarded with such messages.

Another aspect of our journey we learn through sports and other competitive aspects is the whole idea of Mastery. We want to be the best, so we work hard to gain the skills and advantages necessary to propel us to the top. In the journey of life, however, there are some pitfalls. Unfortunately, none of us are truly the masters of our fates, in spite of all the hype we are fed constantly by a world that does not have our best interests in mind.

To be good at something is mastery in the best sense of the term. However, when mastery becomes a tool for conquest, domination and/or exploitation, there are often problems. In our growth to maturity, we often pass from the quadrant of magic to mastery.

Some people vacillate between these two areas for a considerable period of their lives, and some never escape. History is filled with such examples, like Hitler who gravitated to these two areas of life's journey and never seemed to get beyond them. Hopefully, we can progress to the next quadrant, Mindfulness.

Most of our discussion has been focused on this particular quadrant, regarding the meaning of our experience. Generally, people get to a point where they begin to appreciate more fully some of the deeper things of life. These things are difficult to describe or explain, but certainly can be experienced.

Quality becomes more important than scale or quantity: good friends, family, a good night's sleep, time in the garden and so many other things that may have been overlooked in earlier stages of development. These now become relevant to our experience of life. Faithfulness to our own values and the things which make us unique begins to become more evident and more important. As the years pass, the journeys of other people begin to interest us as we discover that we can learn a great deal from the experiences of others. As we go deeper into the meaning of our own experience, we sooner or later cross over into the realm of mystery.

Of course, for us humans, death is the most dominant and pervasive mystery that confronts us. Backing up from that precipice, we find that we are engulfed in the mystery of living, loving, learning and growing. Maybe these things have meaning and maybe they don't. Like a mountain looming in the fog of life, mystery suddenly is painted in sharp relief in the landscape of our mind.

Many people recoil at the intrusion of mystery in their lives and seek escape once again into the territories of magic or mastery. Ultimately, however, we each must face at some moment the awesome mystery of our own expiration. As contradictory as it seems, the real power for effective living comes in embracing the terror of the unknown and letting the wisdom and beauty of our sunset illuminate our lives.

IN THAT TWILIGHT MOMENT
G. Charles Andersen

In that twilight moment, as the night descends

Shall I curse the daylight as it ends

Or look then for my evening star

Beyond the waning light?

Will I discover the beauty of sunset

And the promise of night?

In the setting sun is shone

What perhaps we've always known

But can't comprehend

That the day must end

And the night descend

On the daylight of our lives.

But then beyond the twilights glow,

Past horizons yet to know

Is there a sunrise on some distant shore?

So in the days that yet remain,

Filled with sunshine or with pain,

Shall we look ahead?

Not with fear and dread

But perhaps instead

Let the love light glow within.

For then beyond the twilights glow

Past horizons yet to know

There'll be a sunrise on a distant shore.

So in life's twilight moment, as the night descends

There's no need to curse the daylight as it ends.

   Just look then for your evening star

   Beyond the waning light

And there discover the beauty of sunset

And the promise of night.

So, that's the short tour of the Dharmic Themescape. Figure 2 summarizes most of this fairly clearly. The Themescape provides a conceptual infrastructure to help us engage some relatively important ideas and issues. The next step is to explore how this information can be applied in terms of Soul Solitude.

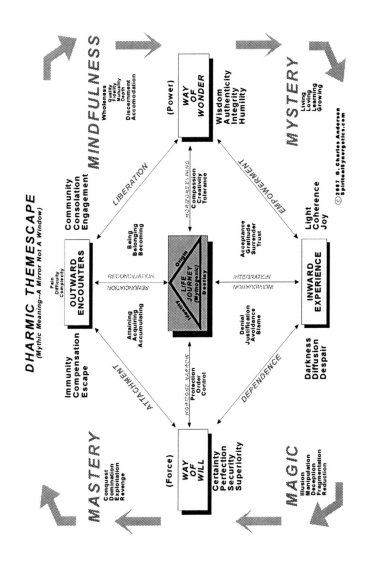

DHARMIC THEMESCAPE
(Mythic Meaning—A Mirror Not A Window)

MINDFULNESS

MYSTERY

MASTERY

MAGIC

WAY OF WONDER (Power)

Wholeness
Quality
Fidelity
Mutuality
Depth
Discernment
Accomodation

Wisdom
Authenticity
Integrity
Humility

Living
Loving
Learning
Growing

© 2007 G. Charles Andersen
Spiritualsynergetics.com

OUTWARD ENCOUNTERS

Pain
Difficulty
Complexity

Community
Consolation
Engagement

Immunity
Compensation
Escape

INWARD EXPERIENCE

Light
Coherence
Joy

Darkness
Diffusion
Despair

WAY OF WILL (Force)

Certainty
Perfection
Security
Superiority

Conquest
Domination
Exploitation
Revenge

Illusion
Manipulation
Deception
Fragmentation
Reduction

LIFE JOURNEY (Mythogenic)

Crisis

Identity

Destiny

Being
Belonging
Becoming

Attaining
Acquiring
Accumulating

Compassion
Creativity
Tolerance

Acceptance
Gratitude
Surrender
Trust

Denial
Justification
Avoidance
Blame

Protection
Order
Control

LIBERATION

EMPOWERMENT

ATTACHMENT

DEPENDENCE

HORIZONS EXPAND

HORIZONS NARROW

RECONCILIATION

RENUNCIATION

INTEGRATION

INDIVIDUATION

APPENDIX THREE:
SOUL CENTERING PRINCIPLES™

Concepts & Process

I.   MINDFULNESS (PRESENCE)

Inward & Outward
a. Stillness (Kenosis)
b. Patience (Non-Judgmental)
c. Focus
      i. Being
      ii. Belonging
      iii. Becoming

II.   ACCEPTANCE

a. Normal
      i. Uncertainty
      ii. Imperfection
      iii. Powerlessness
      iv. Vulnerability
      v. Responsibility (Appropriate/
         Un-inflated)
b. Natural (Sacrament of the Ordinary)
c. Necessary (Unjust)

III. **GRATITUDE**

    a. Blessings (Burdens & Joys)
    b. Gifts (Personal)
    c. Mystery (Sacred-Holy-Real)

IV. **TRUST**

    a. Who We Are
    b. Where We Are
    c. Where We're Going

V. **SURRENDER**

    a. Circumstances
       (Possibilities & Limitations)
    b. Constraints
    c. Challenges
    d. Changes
    e. Choices
    f. Complexity

ABOUT THE AUTHORS

Rhoberta Shaler, PhD, connects people with their authentic selves, their purpose and values, and provides insights and inspiration to overcome the challenges of personal, family and business life. With her, and with the programs she offers, clients uncover the deep parts of themselves that make life meaningful, rich and satisfying. Author of more than a dozen books and audio programs, her most recent book, *Wrestling Rhinos: Conquering Conflict in the Wilds of Work,* has been hailed as "…a business classic." She is the founder of the Optimize! Institute™ in Escondido, CA and Spiritual Living Network™ worldwide. To learn more, visit: Rhoberta.com, OptimizeInstitute.com and SpiritualLivingNetwork.com

G. Charles Andersen, M.A. is a graduate of the renowned Pacifica Graduate Institute with a Masters in Mythological Studies, with an emphasis in depth-psychology. The faculty at Pacifica encouraged him to share his wisdom and insights with a much broader community, outside of academia, which he has done with his writing, workshops and classes. Additionally he has many years of experience working with a broad range of business and church audiences helping them achieve a new vision of themselves and their mission. To learn more, visit: HumanaTeam.com

Rhoberta and Charles are co-founders of the Humana Center in Encinitas, CA where they hold Soul Soulitude seminars and offer other spiritually-enriching experiences.
www.HumanaCenter.com

FURTHER RESOURCES FOR FINDING SOUL SOLITUDE:

The Humana Center

The Humana Center in rustic Encinitas, California is nestled on a rise overlooking the majestic setting of the Pacific Ocean just a few short blocks away. Humana Center participants can experience intimate and intense programs for personal, professional and organizational growth. These programs and Master Classes are specifically designed to provide satisfying depth for the mind, heart and soul.

Based upon the ground-breaking work of co-founders, Rhoberta Shaler, PhD. and G. Charles Andersen, MA, these innovative programs provide a unique synthesis of the mythic, scientific, spiritual and psychological dimensions of life.

Whatever your path, you will undoubtedly find each offering challenges you to new awareness of your journey.

For home study, you can purchase Soul Solitude books, workbooks, audio CDs and music as well. Teleseminars on various topics are also available.

For further information on seminars, products and registration, visit:

www.HumanaCenter.com

We should never lose sight of the fact that
the soul is on a pathway of an endless and
ever-expanding experience and that only by
expansion can it evolve.

- Ernest Holmes

Printed in the United States
117040LV00001B/1-48/A